THINKING THROUGH THE CHILDREN'S SERMON

Thinking Through the Children's Sermon

WILLIAM H. ARMSTRONG

The Pilgrim Press
Cleveland

The Pilgrim Press, 700 Prospect Avenue, Cleveland, Ohio 44115
thepilgrimpress.com

Printed in the United States of America on acid-free paper

11 10 09 08 07 06 5 4 3 2 1

Library of Congress Cataloging-in-Publication Data

Armstrong, William H. (William Howard), 1932–
Thinking through the children's sermon / William H. Armstrong.
p. cm.
Includes bibliographical references.
ISBN-13: 978-0-8298-1733-1 (alk. paper)
1. Preaching to children. I. Title.
BV4235.C4A76 2006
251'.53—dc22 200603013
ISBN-13: 978-0-8298-1733-1
ISBN-10: 0-8298-1733-6

Contents

~

Preface

~

THE CHILDREN KNOW IT IS THEIR TIME, even before the worship leader invites them to come to the front of the church. When the invitation is given, most come eagerly, running or skipping down the aisles, while a few come slowly and reluctantly, looking back to their parents for reassurance. Still others remain in their seats, the younger ones too timid to go with the rest, the older ones feigning indifference but often still listening.

The adults listen too as the leader begins a story or produces some object—a teddy bear, a cereal box, a kite—and uses it to talk to the children. The leader pauses sometimes, seeking responses from the children, or is interrupted by some child's uninhibited remark. The adults may laugh at what the child says or at the leader's discomfort with it, and the leader may turn to make a humorous remark to the congregation.

The talk is brief and soon comes to its conclusion: an affirmation of God's love for every child; an assurance of the goodness of our diversity; a statement that no one is too small to be used by God; or a plea for the environment or some other good cause. And then a brief prayer and the children are directed to their classes or given permission to return to their seats.

That brief interlude in worship, the children's sermon, is more and more common in churches today. Most parishioners have come to accept it and even to welcome it. They sometimes surprise and confound clergy by saying that they get more out of the children's sermon than the one meant for adults. The clergy are like the children: some approach the children's sermon eagerly, others reluctantly, and still others choose to remain in their seats while someone else takes on the task of talking to the children.

Children's sermons are popular, but are they meaningful? Are they edifying or merely entertaining? If they are meaningful and edifying, are they done as well as they might be, with the same prayerful thought and preparation as the sermons given from the pulpit? If not, how might they be improved?

This book is offered as an answer to those questions, telling why I think children's sermons can be both meaningful and edifying and suggesting ways to prepare and present them that will help make them the valuable additions to worship I think they can be. I write as a parish pastor who preached hundreds of children's sermons, often without the time to think deeply about their purpose or methods, but who now, in retirement, has had the time to reflect on those sermons and on the sermons of others. These are my reflections, given with the hope that they may be useful to those who talk to children in worship and to the children themselves.

> A word about the name "children's sermon": The word "sermon" seems too weighty to be used with children; even adults are often intimidated by it. Many churches prefer to call the time spent with the children during worship something like "children's chat," "children's moment," or "children's message," and that is entirely reasonable. Nevertheless, I have used the name "children's sermon" here for two reasons. First, it is the most commonly used name and is easily recognizable. Second, it serves as a reminder that our talks to children are what any sermon is at its best: an attempt in our own words to speak God's Word to God's people.

To speak about the "children's sermon," however, leads inevitably to speaking about "preaching to children" with its unpleasant suggestion of lecturing them. Jay T. Stocking rightly deplored preaching that lectures children and laid down this rule for speaking to them: "Thou shalt not be *preachy* in manner, in word, in tone of voice, or in anything else that thou doest. . . . Children hear all the 'preaching' that they can well endure, at home and in school. . . ."[1]

My hope is that we can fulfill our calling of preaching the Gospel to children simply by talking to them, usually seriously, sometimes playfully, always respectfully, in ways that no one but the clergy will think of as "preaching to children."

Introduction

Why Children's Sermons?

~

NOT EVERYONE WELCOMES CHILDREN in worship services. Some consider them a distraction and prefer that they spend the worship hour elsewhere, in a nursery or in classes where they can learn and worship with children their own age. But more and more churches are encouraging parents to bring their children to worship with them, believing that children too are part of the household of God and that they learn to worship by being with the worshiping congregation.

That is how I learned to worship, sitting next to my parents and my grandmother—a minister's daughter—and surrounded by some of my neighbors and teachers, our doctor, our grocer, our banker, and the man who brought our mail. Their evident trust and devotion nurtured my trust and devotion, and I began to experience the other realities of worship: awe, reverence, love, hope, gratitude, contrition.

To be sure, there was much I did not understand; a child comes to understand religious matters slowly. But my parents were right to teach me by immersing me in worship. Children learn by participation. Many of us take our children with us to baseball games, and not much is understood at first. What child understands the infield fly rule or the definition of a balk or how to calculate an earned run average? Yet they learn to sing "Take Me Out to the Ball Game," and they enjoy the peanuts and Cracker Jack. They bring their gloves, hoping to join the game themselves by catching a ball; they come to admire the heroes of the game; and they gain a love for the game and gradually come to understand the thing they love. It is just that way with children in the church at worship.

Still, some who agree with that and encourage children to participate in worship are nonetheless skeptical of the children's sermon. Why devote a few minutes to the children's sermon instead of involving the children in the whole service? they ask. Why not have them serve as greeters, acolytes, and ushers? Read scripture, write prayers, make banners, sing, act in plays, and lead readings? Why not, indeed? Children not only can learn about worship by participating in it; they also can make their own contribution to the worship service by the parts they play and by the spontaneity, wonder, openness, trust, and joy they share with the congregation.

But one lengthy part of the service defies any easy participation by most children: the sermon.

If a sermon based on the Bible is to be meaningful for adults, it must deal with theology, either explicitly or implicitly—creation, sin, grace, revelation, incarnation, atonement, providence, the problem of evil, death and the life to come—and with adult subjects in relation to theology—marriage, divorce, sexism, racism, education, leisure, war, the relation of church and state, the ethics of the workplace. And to do those things, the sermon must use adult thoughts, adult language, and adult arguments. I will contend that we often underestimate children's experience and thoughtfulness, but they are still not able to understand the mature thought adults should be wrestling with in the sermon.

Children also have their own concerns that need to be addressed. Religious holidays, overly familiar to many adults, are new to children and of great interest. The world of nature is also new to them and full of wonders. School is uppermost in their minds. Most of a child's life is spent in school with its successes and failures, its friendships, its teasing and bullying. And then there are those concerns that seem so insignificant to adults and so important to children: rejection by someone who had been considered a friend; not being chosen for a play or a team; being picked on by older brothers and sisters; not being able to make their own decisions—even about what clothes to wear; knowing when to tell on someone and when not to tell; being punished with the class for one child's misdeeds; making mistakes they are sure will ruin their lives.

We easily dismiss those childish concerns, but they are real to the children. Hans Christian Andersen understood how deeply they are felt. One of his stories tells of some children who buried a dead lap dog, stood up a beer bottle as a tombstone, and then charged the other children one button to see the grave. One little girl tried to peek in at the gate but did not have a button and so didn't get to see the grave. She stood outside the gate all afternoon and "then she burst out crying and, hiding her eyes in her little sunburned hands, she sat down upon the ground. She alone, of all the children in the street, had not seen the little lap dog's grave! Now that was grief, a sorrow as sharp as a grownup's can be!"[1]

Children's concerns are intensely important to them. How will they be addressed?

Some Christian educators, Carolyn Brown among them, agree that children need to hear God's Word in worship but think both children and adults can be addressed in what is called the "real sermon," without the use of what Brown calls "pint-sized sermons." She would make the "real" sermons "child-friendly" by bearing in mind that children are listening and by including such things as stories from childhood and children's classics as illustrations. These "carefully planted tidbits," she believes, will catch the children's interest even if they do not understand everything in the sermon.[2]

But the purpose of illustrations in sermons is to illustrate, to shed light on some larger idea that may be difficult for adults to understand without the help of the illustration. Children may recognize and remember an illustration that comes from childhood or a child's book but may have no idea why it was told, and in that case little has been gained beyond the feeling of inclusion given to them by hearing a familiar story. At other times, a story is told, not to illustrate, but to carry a message of its own. Children may understand that kind of story but, again, may have no idea why it was included in the sermon.

If you are reading this because you are a preacher, and if children are present when you are preaching to adults, recognize the children's presence, include them in your remarks, and let them gain what they can from the sermon, but consider giving them something of their own, too, in a separate children's sermon. That sermon will be an opportunity to provide children with a well-rounded message fashioned specifically for them rather than "tidbits" from a message meant primarily for others, an opportunity for them to hear God's Word at their level of understanding, in their language, and addressed to their concerns.

People argue for the children's sermon by saying it will make the children feel included and valued by the congregation, leaving them with a positive attitude toward the church; that it will build rapport between them and the pastor; that the time devoted to them in worship will demonstrate that God has time for them, too. Those are, indeed, benefits of the children's sermon, but I advocate it mainly so that there is a time during worship when children can be engaged by God's Word in words and ways they are capable of understanding.

That can be done in more than one way; there is no single approach or method for presenting children's sermons. Each method has its advantages and disadvantages, and I describe and evaluate those methods in part three of this book. But first I take a long look at the children who will hear our message and at the message itself.

PART ONE: CHILDREN

~ 1 ~

Children's Thoughts

The children we address are limited in experience with life and with language, and those limitations make it difficult for them to understand sermons intended for adults. Nevertheless, we often underestimate the life experiences they do have and how deeply they think about those experiences. This can lead us to shortchange them when we come to address them in children's sermons, too often patronizing them with our shallow stunts and stories.

We like to think of children as innocent, living cloudless lives, unaware of life's realities, presenting to us new and clean slates on which we can write the truths of life. But that innocence is a myth. Some of them have already experienced failure, perhaps having been held back in school and separated from their friends in the process. A good many have seen their parents divorce; they are being shuffled back and forth between two homes and may be adapting to step-parents and new siblings. Some may have parents in prison; some may be living with foster parents; some may know more about addiction than the pastor does; some may be ashamed of their families. It is not unusual for children to feel gnawing guilt, often for ills they only imagine they are responsible for. Many children are living in fear: fear of getting lost, of strangers, of bullies, of being mocked for bed-wetting, of failing to meet their parents' expectations, of replacement by a new baby, of always being the last one chosen, of nightmares, of violence and abuse at home—nightmares that come in the daytime, as one author describes them.[1] An old book expresses these concerns well in its title: *Big Problems on Little Shoulders*.[2]

Children wonder about those things, think deeply about them, try to make sense of them. And they wonder about life itself and what it means. Robert Coles, the Harvard psychiatrist, describes them as asking the same questions Paul Gauguin was asking when he titled one of his paintings, "Where Do We Come From? What Are We? Where Are We Going?" Coles says they ask those eternal questions "more intensely, unremittingly, and subtly than we sometimes imagine."[3]

Robert Louis Stevenson saw little difference between children and adults in their thoughts about life. He writes that "children think very much the same thoughts and dream the same dreams, as bearded men and marriageable women."[4]

A similar view of childhood was held by Henry Wadsworth Longfellow. When he was in his late thirties, Longfellow visited his hometown of Portland, Maine, a visit that later led him to contemplate his childhood in the poem "My Lost Youth." There he reflects on his early friendships and dreams:

> I remember the gleams and glooms that dart
> Across the school-boy's brain;
> The song and the silence in the heart. . . .

He ends each verse of the poem with this refrain: "And the thoughts of youth are long, long thoughts."[5] They are indeed.

When Ronald Knox, the Catholic scholar and translator of the New Testament, was four years old, he was asked what he liked to do. He replied: "I think all day, and at night I think about the past."[6] Bertrand Russell writes that when he was alone as a child he "used to wander about the garden, alternately collecting birds' eggs and meditating on the flight of time"—the kind of meditation that he thought is "never mentioned to adults."[7]

A writer better known a century ago than now, John Townsend Trowbridge, describes the thoughts he had in childhood:

> The world was all a mystery to me, which I was forever seeking to solve; but the greatest mystery of all was that of the people around me. I can hardly remember a time when I did not try to enter somehow into their consciousness and think with their thoughts. I would sit patiently in my little chair, and watch my mother rocking and knitting, something within me yearning to fathom something in her; wondering how it seemed to be as old as she, how life looked to her, and what it was that made her chair rock and her hands move, always just so, and not otherwise. When I was old enough to be taken to meeting, I would entertain myself by studying certain persons whose faces fascinated me, endeavoring to guess their secrets, and make out why one was gray and wrinkled, another young and handsome, and why one was always so distinctly one's own self and not another's. I knew they never had any such thoughts as troubled a little boy like me, but what *were* their thoughts?[8]

Walter De la Mare tells of a girl seven and a half years old who confided to her father:

"Sometimes I think about things. I think t-h-u-m-b spells thumb and t-h-i-n-g spells thing, and *why* should they spell thumb and thing? Why shouldn't they spell something else? And then I think two from six leaves four, and two from eight leaves six, and why shouldn't they leave three or something else? And when I think like this I get all puzzled."[9]

Sarah, the four-year-old daughter of philosophy professor Gareth B. Matthews, asked him how their cat got fleas. His answer, that the cat got them from another cat, led to a further question: "How did *that* cat get fleas?" When he said that the fleas must have come from still another cat, Sarah said: "But Daddy, it can't go on like that forever; the only thing that goes on and on like that forever is numbers!"[10]

After noting the thinking of many such children, Matthews concludes that "for many young members of the human race, philosophical thinking—including, on occasion, subtle and ingenious reasoning—is as natural as making music and playing games, and quite as much a part of being human."[11]

Perhaps not every child thinks that deeply, but I suspect that many more do so than we imagine. Those with thoughts like that may be disappointed if what we offer them on Sunday mornings is too shallow, too *childish*. Imagine the chagrin of the child who has been pondering causality and infinity if a children's sermon begins—as one published sermon suggests: "Do you know what this is? (*Hold up an apple and wait for responses.*)"[12] We fail the children if we feed them with neither the meat nor the milk the Bible speaks about,[13] but only cotton candy in a religious wrapper.

Children's thoughts are not only long in the sense of deep but also are often long-lasting as well. Bertrand Russell, writing his autobiography in his nineties, still resented having been treated unjustly when he was four years old. A photographer had promised him a sponge cake if he would sit still for a photograph and Russell eagerly did as he was told, but the photographer never kept his promise.[14]

Paul Steinberg, a German Jew who as a child had drifted with his family through four different countries in the 1930s, ended up in Paris, where he experienced his first racist attack. There, "right in the middle of study hall," one of his teachers called him *heimatlos*, "homeless, stateless, in other words, human rubbish. I was absolutely furious, and helpless. What can you do when you're eleven years old? You can remember." And six decades later he still remembered the incident, "as though it were yesterday."[15]

In her book *Growing Together*, Anne Rupp writes about a middle-aged chaplain who said that, when he was about eight years old, his father was repairing a car and asked for a wrench. He gave his father the wrong wrench, and the father said, "Can't you do anything right?" After a moment, the chaplain added: "Those words have haunted me all my life!"[16]

My father in his later years often thought about a question he had asked as a boy. One winter, he began to wonder what happened to the grass under the snow. Would it all die? Would it all dry up and blow away when the snow melted? Would the ground be bare with no grass? But when he asked about it, people would laugh at him or give him answers he didn't trust. He had to wait until spring to find out. He promised himself that if he grew up and had little boys he would never laugh at their questions; instead, he would give them the right answers or admit that he didn't know the answers. That little incident and his reflections on it affected his whole life—and mine as well.

"The thoughts of youth are long, long thoughts"—which is perhaps one reason Jesus stressed the significance of "every careless word [we] utter."[17]

A child's thoughts are deeper and longer-lasting than we may imagine but, because of inexperience, they are also often confused. My step-grandfather's birthday was February 21. He used to tease me by saying he was one day older than George Washington. I knew from drawing all those hatchets and cherries in school that Washington's birthday was February 22, so what my grandfather told me seemed to be true, yet I had a nagging feeling that somehow it couldn't be right. Much later I discovered that he had been born more than a hundred years after Washington, and still later I learned that an understanding of chronology develops slowly in most children.

My best friend lived across the street in our small Ohio town. Sometimes he would tell me that he was going with his family to visit relatives in Poland. I was always puzzled when he came back a few days later or even the same day. I thought Poland was much farther away than that. Long afterward, I learned that there was a town named Poland in Ohio and that was where his relatives lived. Another thing that puzzled me was Labor Day. I thought "labor" meant "work," and yet all the adults I knew stayed home from work that day. I was thinking hard about those things, trying to understand them, but I had not yet experienced enough of life to think them through.

I was not the only child whose thoughts were confused. As a boy, Charles Dickens studied the catechism in the Book of Common Prayer, where he learned that he "should keep God's holy will and commandments, and walk in the same all the days of my life." But he thought that "to walk in the same all the days of my life" obliged him "always to go through the town from our house in one particular direction, and never to vary it by turning down by the wheelwright's or up by the mill."[18]

Kenneth Grahame was a little more successful in overcoming his childhood puzzlement. He had heard someone say that "all roads lead to Rome." "I had taken the remark very seriously, of course," he said, "and puzzled over it many days." But he couldn't see how it could be true and finally concluded that "there must have been some mistake."[19]

Children think, often deeply, but their lack of experience may result in thoughts that are incomplete and unsatisfying without some help from sympathetic adults.

~ 2 ~
Children's Thoughts about Religion

WHAT IS TRUE OF CHILDREN'S thought in general is also true of their thinking about religion. They often think deeply about religious matters even if they do not always have enough experience to reach satisfying conclusions. That girl carrying her doll with her to the front of the church, the boy tucking his yo-yo in his pocket on his way down the aisle and having difficulty gathering in the string, may have thought more deeply about religious matters than you can imagine. It may have been just such a child who said to an interviewer: "In the parish church I was always listening carefully, thinking and pondering about what we were saying and having said to us."[1]

In his tragedy *Faust*, Goethe depicts an evil spirit reminding the guilt-ridden Gretchen about her childhood in this way:

> How different it was with you, Gretchen,
> When you, still full of innocence,
> Came here to the altar,
> Prattling prayers
> Out of your worn little book,
> Half child's play,
> Half God in your heart.[2]

Half child's play and half God in the heart—this is a good description of the lives of many children. Robert Coles convinced me through his studies of childhood that many children, playful as they are, think seriously about spiritual matters. He describes one ten-year-old girl with no religious affiliation who said: "Just because you don't go to church and don't believe what they tell you [there] doesn't mean you don't think about God, and about how you should be good, and what are the really big things in life, and the things that don't make any difference. I can sit and look out the window, and I'll watch it snow; and I believe in God then. So does my mommy; she says each snowflake is different from every other snowflake that ever was and ever will be, and that shows you there's something out there that makes our world so special."

Coles sees children as seekers who again and again have "thought long and hard about who God is [and] about what God might be like."[3] He quotes Dorothy Day in support of his conclusions about the spiritual life of children: "I . . . remember all the *wondering* I did, all the questions I had about life and God and the purpose of things. . . . I don't think it's been any different with my daughter [Tamar], or with the many children I've known during my life; they all want to know why they are here, and what's ahead as they get older—heaven, hell, nothing at all, or as Tamar once said to me, 'Mother, will it be the cemetery, and that's the end?'"[4]

The stories of many other children demonstrate their early thoughts about religion. When Saint Thérèse of Lisieux was a child in an abbey school, one of the nuns asked her what she did with her free time. She said that "she hid herself between her bed and the wall, she pulled the curtain round her, and she thought." When the nun asked her what she thought about, she replied, "about God, about life, about eternity." And the nun laughed at her.[5]

John Trowbridge says: "I was always wondering at the beauty and mystery of the earth and sky,—the air in its place, the water in its place, the birds adapted to their life, the fishes to theirs, the growth of trees and grass and flowers, the sun by day, and by night the moon and stars; and I never once imagined that these visible miracles could have come about by any sort of chance."[6]

Albert Schweitzer showed an unusual religious insight in his earliest years. Even before he began school, he couldn't understand why he should pray only for humans. "So," he writes:

> when my mother had prayed with me and had kissed me good-night, I used to add silently a prayer that I had composed myself for all living creatures. It ran thus: 'O, heavenly Father, protect and bless all things that have breath; guard them from all evil, and let them sleep in peace.'[7]

He also wondered about things he read in the Bible. How could Jesus' parents have been poor after they received such expensive gifts from the wise men? What did they do with the gifts? "And that the Wise Men should never have troubled themselves again about the Child Jesus was to me incomprehensible." Those and other childhood experiences led the mature Schweitzer to conclude that "much more goes on in a child's heart than others are allowed to suspect."[8]

In addition to their thoughts about religion, children have religious experiences that can have a lifelong influence. Edward Hoffman's *Visions of Innocence: Spiritual and Inspirational Experiences of Childhood* and Edward Robinson's *The Original Vision: A Study of the Religious Experience of Childhood* present example after example of adults relating religious experiences from their childhood, experiences that often had never been shared with anyone. Some of the experiences appear to be influenced by Christianity, others are mystical or pantheistic, but all brought the children into touch with things transcendent.[9]

Consider the retired Californian, raised in a non-religious household in Pittsburgh, who remembers playing in her grandmother's backyard when she was five. As she was looking at some roses, she "suddenly felt God's presence in an almost overpowering way. The 'trigger' could partly have been the sheer beauty of the roses, but something else must have lifted my being into a new realm of awareness." From that brief experience, she became a lifelong believer in

God. "Fifty-seven years have passed," she said, "and I still remember this experience quite clearly."[10]

A mother in Israel described herself to another researcher as fully secular and said she had never spoken to her daughter about God. Yet at two years old the girl began to tell her about God's wonders. "He created the animals and the sky and the earth," she said and went into detail about the creation. Her surprised mother asked her how she knew these things, and the girl replied, "Because God told me."[11]

Even without clear thoughts about religion or memorable religious experiences, children experience the awe and wonder that underlie religious thought and experience. It may be wonder at the world they find themselves in. A young girl new to the North Dakota sky wrote: "The sky is full of blue / and full of the mind of God."[12] Or it may be wonder at the notion of a God beyond this world. Walt Whitman reflects on his childhood amazement at discussions of God in a little poem called "A Child's Amaze:"

> Silent and amazed even when a little boy,
> I remember I heard the preacher every Sunday put God in
> his statements,
> As contending against some being or influence.[13]

Children also know the trust that underlies religion, even though they may not be able to articulate it. And they have a keen sense of the justice that Christians attribute to God. Calvin Trillin says that his third-grade daughter's "eye for injustice was already so sharp that she was referred to as the Amnesty International representative at our house."[14]

Children do not come to us with clean slates waiting for us to write things like "religion" or "God" on them. They have already thought about those things, and may already have reached conclusions about them. Ana-Maria Rizzuto, a psychoanalyst who has studied the formation of children's conceptions of God, puts it in this striking way: "No child arrives at the 'house of God' without his pet God under his arm."[15]

~ 3 ~
Respect for Children

WHAT ALL THIS SAYS TO ME IS THAT there is an unexpected depth to children and that we need to address them with respect for their budding thoughts and faith. In fact, one of the main things needed for anyone attempting children's sermons is respect for children themselves. As Juvenal puts it in a different context, "The greatest respect is owed to a child."[1]

There is a wonderful photograph of Albert Schweitzer taken by Nat Fein during Schweitzer's only visit to the United States. In the picture, he is greeting a little girl who is holding a doll in one hand. Her other hand is in his large hand, and he is kneeling on one knee, talking to her face to face, with all his attention focused on her. The picture is a good symbol of the kind of respect that is fitting for all of us who deal with children.

This respect may be shown by physically getting down to the children's level as Schweitzer did, although doing that depends on one's physical limitations and on the nature of the setting. Respect can be shown to the children who gather on Sundays in other ways as well: by waiting for the young girl who is still slowly finding her way down the aisle when the others are all assembled; by making sure that each child has a place to sit; by learning the children's names and addressing them by name; by talking to them person to person and not as someone in authority over them; by not rushing in to fill the silence when a child is slowly reaching for an idea; by taking their ideas seriously, no matter how limited the ideas are; by showing the same interest in the children outside the sanctuary as when we are "on stage" with them during worship. We can, in James Whitcomb Riley's homespun words:

Treat 'em right and reco'nize
Human souls is all one size.[2]

By showing the children respect, we may be rewarded by receiving their respect in return and their attention to what we have to say. Parker Rossman noticed a little girl paying close attention to a sermon. After the service, he asked her if there was something about it that especially interested her. After thinking a moment, she said: "No, I always listen to him, because he always listens to me."[3]

~ 4 ~

Deepening Our Understanding of Children

If an understanding of children is necessary for us to speak to them and if our understanding seems inadequate, how can we deepen it? Those with children of their own have the advantage of watching their children grow and develop, but even parents may feel the need to learn more than they already know about children.

A good deal can be learned from the study of child development, especially about the stages of development that all children go through—physically, mentally, morally, emotionally, and spiritually—and the way speech and comprehension develop from the concrete to the abstract. Those concepts help to clarify what can be expected of the children of different ages who appear before us on Sunday morning. Several useful books have summarized the current understanding of child development and emphasized its importance for those who preach children's sermons, in particular, O. Suthern Sims Jr.'s *Creating and Leading Children's Sermons: A Developmental Approach* and Sara Covin Juengst's *Sharing Faith with Children: Rethinking the Children's Sermon.*[1]

Like Sims and Juengst, most recent writers on children's sermons have been heavily influenced by the conclusions of students of child development, and most recommend that we limit ourselves to what scholars have determined to be "age-appropriate" subjects and methods with children. Gareth B. Matthews, however, who has held philosophical dialogues with children, questions the dominant theories of developmental psychologists about children's thinking, saying that young children have an unsuspected capacity to think philosophically and discuss the basic questions of life. His *Dialogues with Children*, for example, shows eight- to eleven-year-old children responding well to much more challenging modes of thought than are found in most children's sermons.[2] Nor is Matthews alone in his thinking. The Institute for the Advancement of Philosophy for Children at Montclair State University has enough confidence in children's thinking to offer a complete curriculum for the study of philosophy in elementary as well as secondary schools.

But one does not need to be an expert in either child development or the philosophy of childhood to understand children. It is instructive simply to get to know them, if not one's own, then children in church school or the public schools or on the playground. In recent years, my wife and I volunteered in a kindergarten class in an urban public school, and that has given me not only a better understanding of the young child but also a reminder of what it is like to spend a major part of one's day in school.[3]

If you want to deepen your understanding of children, talk to them wherever you meet them, ask them questions—about their pets or their friends or their schoolwork—enter into the world of their imagination, and *listen* to them. Henry Wadsworth Longfellow set a good example once when he was visiting a friend. Hearing his friend's young daughters laughing in the hall, Longfellow asked to see them. The girls were overawed by Longfellow's gray hair and beard but attracted by his smile and then won over entirely when he asked them: "Where are your dolls? I want you to show me your dolls! Not the fine ones you keep for company, but those you love best and play with every day." Soon they were showing him their "shabby little favorites with battered noses, and were eagerly telling him their names and histories, while he questioned them with an interest that wholly won their childish hearts."[4]

Abraham Lincoln also knew how to enter a child's world. A

Springfield, Illinois, neighbor said that Lincoln "took uncommon pains to remember the faces and names of children," making use "of every chance for pleasant, mostly whimsical conversation with the young, and he entered, as few men have the knack of doing, into their small concerns, easily winning their confidence."[5]

Memoirs can be another source of understanding. Some authors of memoirs simply describe the circumstances of their childhood, but the more perceptive authors shed light on childhood by telling how they thought and felt as children. Here, for example, is June Jordan reflecting on worshiping at St. Phillip's Episcopal Church in Brooklyn in her memoir, *Soldier: A Poet's Childhood*:

> It was so quiet!
>
> There were no arguments, no cigars, no sarcasm, no jangling oddities or dangers.
>
> I felt safe.
>
> Everyone stayed on company behavior, or better than that.
>
> And the stupendous height and depth of the church imparted a sense of infinite, imperturbable shelter.
>
> . . . A good part of the time I was not sure what anybody was talking about, but no one seemed to care about that:
>
> What mattered was the magical language and its repetition that left you feeling united and taken care of, and happy "in the Lord."[6]

And here is Maryse Condé talking about her mother in her memoir, *Tales from the Heart*: "My mother expected too much from me. I was perpetually required to be the best in everything and everywhere. Consequently, I lived in fear of disappointing her. My terror was hearing that unequivocal judgment she too often sentenced me with: 'You'll never do anything worthwhile with your life!'"[7]

Other recent memoirs that provided me with insights into the way children think and feel include Julia Collins's *My Father's War: A Memoir* and Yolanda Young's *On Our Way to Beautiful: A Family Memoir*. Older books, too, such as Charles Dickens's *My Early Times*, Lucy

Larcom's *A New England Girlhood*, Bertrand Russell's *Autobiography*, and Albert Schweitzer's *Memoirs of Childhood and Youth* have also been helpful, as has George Orwell's insightful essay on his childhood, "Such, Such Were the Joys . . ."—which begins with his early prayer: "Please God, do not let me wet my bed!"[8]

Some authors relate insights about childhood through fiction rather than memoir. Consider this striking passage from Herman Melville's *Redburn*:

> Talk not of the bitterness of middle-age and after life; a boy can feel all that, and much more, when upon his young soul the mildew has fallen; and the fruit, which with others is only blasted after ripeness, with him is nipped in the first blossom and bud. And never again can such blights be made good; they strike in too deep, and leave such a scar that the air of Paradise might not erase it.[9]

The blight Melville speaks of is abundantly portrayed in both fact and fiction: poverty, abuse, abandonment, despair. But so are the joys: the friendships, the dreams, the discoveries, and the wonder of childhood.

It is also instructive to read the books children read. Don't read only those that the educators recommend; study the well-worn books the children bring you, asking you to "read it again." Pay attention, too, to the programs they watch on television, the songs they sing; and the games they play. Seek out the people who work regularly with children, the Christian educators, the elementary school teachers, and the children's librarians in our congregations and communities who, if we ask for their help, can be our best allies in our efforts to learn about children.

We can also reflect on our own childhood. Antoine De Saint-Exupéry says in the dedication to *The Little Prince*, "All grown-ups were children first. (But few of them remember it.)"[10] Those who make an effort to remember how they thought and felt as children will be better able to understand those who are children now. And the children will be receptive to the honest recollections of our childhood that we share with them: the mistakes we made and the lessons we learned.

To share our reflections on our childhood is to assume that our experiences are similar to those of the children. I am convinced that they are similar, that human nature remains unchanged from generation to generation. We share common human experiences with the children just as we both share experiences with the people who lived in biblical times, which is what allows us to preach about those people and enables the children to understand what we say about them.

But even though human nature is unchanging, the circumstances of our lives are always changing, and those changes affect the ways we think and feel. Just as some of us were deeply marked as children by living through the Cold War or the war in Vietnam, today's children are marked by living in an age of terrorism with its new realities of suicide bombings, beheadings, and preemptive war. Those things will profoundly affect children's lives—especially in this day of instant communication—making them fearful of things they hear about but cannot possibly understand, making them wary of people they may not even know, and making them aware, perhaps for the first time, that there are things and people from whom their parents cannot protect them. They are, in the words of a book about children written in response to the terrorist attacks on September 11, 2001, *Living with the Boogeyman.*[11]

If we are to understand children today, we need to be aware of our constantly changing world and of the fears and anxieties those changes sometimes create in children. Fortunately, we have an opportunity in our children's sermons to reassure them, in the words of a popular song, that "God Is Bigger than the Boogeyman."[12]

PART TWO: MESSAGE

~ 5 ~

More Than a Lesson

THE CHILDREN'S SERMON IS SOMETIMES thought of as a lesson, as information to be imparted, as something to be taught and learned. Ministers are often advised to use the children's sermon to make children familiar with the church building; to teach about hymns, prayers, and the other parts of the liturgy; to explain words used in church services; to acquaint them with the church year; to introduce them to the church budget or its officers; or to tell them about people in the Bible. But the children's sermon is more than a lesson.

Suppose that someone should speak to the children about the twelve disciples. The preacher might name the disciples and give their occupations. A vivid presentation might convey their clothing, their calling, and their varied characters. The more attentive listeners might come away knowing more than many adults about Jesus' followers. I can even imagine a bright youngster being inspired to go home and memorize the names of the twelve and proudly reciting them to the pastor the next Sunday.

That, to me, would be an interesting lesson but not yet a children's sermon; it would be teaching rather than preaching. What would be missing is the challenge to personal involvement—in this case, Jesus' call to these listening children to become disciples too. This is the kind of appeal Albert Schweitzer describes in the conclusion to his

Quest of the Historical Jesus: "He comes to us as One unknown, without a name, as of old, by the lake-side, He came to those men who knew Him not. He speaks to us the same word: 'Follow thou me!'"[1]

The personal element could easily be included. It might be as simple a thing as a brief game of "Simon Says" followed by a game of "Jesus Says" with examples of the things Jesus challenges us to do and be. Information about the original disciples could be included in a children's sermon, but the point of a sermon is not their discipleship but ours.

We can learn from hymns. The words of hymns often do what sermons ought to do—bring us into a personal relationship with the biblical stories. Consider "We are climbing Jacob's ladder" or "Were you there when they crucified my Lord?" Or:

What can I give Him,
Poor as I am?
If I were a shepherd
I would bring a lamb,
If I were a wise man
I would do my part,—
Yet what I can I give Him,
Give my heart.[2]

The question that ought always to be on our minds as we prepare to speak to children is: What relationship does the biblical text have to these children? How can it speak to them? How can it speak to Damon, whose mother is always hovering over him, so anxious is she to have him succeed; to Patty, whom the boys call "Fatty Patty," not just behind her back but to her face; to Chrystal, who is in love with dance and revels in the attention she receives for her graceful ways; to Luke, whose family just moved to the trailer park outside town and who will start a new school on Monday; to Carrie, whose brother is seriously ill with cancer and whose parents are so absorbed with his illness that she calls herself "the invisible girl"; to Adam, who sat in that front pew only last month for his "Grampy's" funeral; to Emily, who is excited about being a flower girl when her daddy marries her new stepmother; to Derek, who emptied his piggy bank to help buy goats for people in some other country (he can't remember where); to John, who always covers his bulletin with pictures of space ships, missiles, and explosions?

How could the text speak to the boy Fred Craddock tells about? The boy was so excited because his father had promised him a calf to be all his own. But the day the calf was born, he came home from school to find it dead. In church the next Sunday, in the midst of all the affirmations of God's goodness, he could only think, "But my calf is dead."[3]

Or how could the text speak to Dorie? A young girl in Tennessee drew a picture of another girl for Robert Coles and titled it "Dorie, the girl nobody loved."[4]

The minister who is using clever little puppets to talk about the twelve disciples and their occupations may be of little help to these children.

Ask yourself how the meaning of your text can be brought to bear on the lives of the children before you—not "the children" as a group, but these individual children: the Damons, Pattys, and Dories of your congregation. How can your text speak to the things that matter to them? to their dreams and disappointments? to their joys and fears? How can it help them find meaning in their lives? How can it deepen their relationship with God? How can it help them experience God's presence in this moment? The answers to those questions will point our messages in the right direction.

~ 6 ~

Sharing the Faith

I ASSUME THAT OUR SERMONS will have a biblical basis, that we are not merely moralizing or passing on cultural values such as politeness, perseverance, honesty, and self-esteem, nor just teaching children about the church, but that we are passing on the stories of our faith. And I assume that those stories are as relevant to children as they are to adults. Of course, the theological terms adults use with the stories will not be understood, but the reality behind them will be. "Creation" may mean little to a child, but the many wonders of this world excite thoughts of the Creator in people of all ages. "Atonement" is not a word to be used with children, but children will understand what it means to be forgiven and to be once again on good terms with God. The word "providence" is probably meaningless to a child, but a God who provides for us like a good parent will be readily understood. "Incarnation" will mean nothing to most children, but Jesus, the Word become flesh, may come to mean everything.

The task of the preacher is to share the faith as we know it—God's love for us, the good news of forgiveness through Christ, the abiding presence of God's Spirit—and to share our own love for God and our passion for God's ways. But how can that best be done? It will probably not be done well if we go from week to week searching for "something to say to the children," even if the search begins before Saturday night. It requires a plan.

For many people, the plan is the lectionary, the scripture readings that many denominations assign for each Sunday and that provide the texts for preaching. The advantage of using the lectionary is that it ensures a systematic presentation of the Christian message throughout the church year. It frees us from the necessity of searching for topics for the children's sermon and ensures that our children's sermons will complement the main sermons and fit into the overall themes of the services. The disadvantage of using the lectionary is that the lessons have been chosen with adults in mind, and some of them are simply too difficult for children or too remote from their experience.

I think the lectionary is a good plan to follow in order to convey the fullness of the biblical message. The varied lessons challenge us to find the relationship between the many facets of scripture and the many facets of childhood. But I also think it is sensible to abandon any Sunday's lessons that seem to have no clear relevance to children. Perhaps another text that relates to the theme of the service could be used instead. I would also not hesitate to abandon the lectionary when some event that affects the children needs to be addressed. This might be something as ordinary as the beginning of school or something as unusual as a tornado, the outbreak of a war, or the death of someone close to them.

Susan Johnson tells about an eight-year-old child in the community who was hit and killed by a drunk driver. Three weeks later, as Johnson was concluding her children's sermon, another eight-year-old raised her hand. "Next week," she asked, "will you talk about drunk driving?"[1]

One children's sermon fittingly celebrated the death of a friend of the children. Kenny, a high school student born with Down syndrome, was a faithful member of his church, greeting people in the narthex each Sunday and carrying the cross in the procession as often as he could. With the mental age of a six-year-old, he also sat with the children during the children's sermon. When Kenny died of cardiac arrest at seventeen, the following Sunday's children's sermon naturally became a time to talk about his life and to thank God for it.[2]

Still, on an ordinary Sunday, the children's sermon ought to relate to the scripture used, whether from the lectionary or not, or to the theme of the day. It does not have to relate directly to the sermon for adults, but it may do so—telling a story, for example, that then becomes the basis for an extended meditation with the adults, or in some other way introducing or illustrating the subject of the adult sermon.[3] In any case, relating the children's sermon to the scripture or worship theme or adult sermon means planning for the children's sermon at the same time as the rest of the service is planned.

What about using sermons from the many published collections of children's sermons? Some of them are solidly based on the scriptures. Many of them contain creative ideas and techniques, and they are prepared so that they are, as one author describes them, "ready-to-go."[4] Is it legitimate to use them?

Those books are useful for seeing what other preachers are doing and useful for stimulating our own thinking. But preaching, whether to adults or to children, always must be directed to a unique situation. It is this preacher speaking to this congregation in this community on this Sunday morning. And no one else is in a position to prepare that message for us, not even those accomplished authors who have published their children's sermons. I once included in a sermon to adults a long reading that I thought said some eloquent things. Afterward, a wise friend gently chided me, saying that he came to church to hear what his pastor in his church had to say, not what someone else had to say to people in some other situation. And he was right. Secondhand sermons, like secondhand clothes, usually don't fit.

The best children's sermons are those in which we share our own understanding of the faith with the children and do it in our own way. One that stands out in my mind was given by a young hospital chaplain who was filling the pulpit during the pastor's vacation. He sat facing the few children who were there that day, showed them an old suitcase, and told them about a trip he took as a child. Very simply he told the children how much his faith in God meant to him during the difficulties of that trip and how much it meant to him now. He spoke as one might speak to a friend, heart to heart, with no condescension, no cleverness, and without "performing." And the children, who like all children understand sincerity and respect even if they don't understand everything that is said, "heard him gladly."

Stan Stewart and Pauline Hubner state the approach in this way: "The concerns and cares that you have are, more often than not, those of the children in your life and in your church. . . . Be sure that what is and has been important to you in your life, is a rich resource for 'Talking about Something Important.'"[5]

And Fred Rogers—Mr. Rogers—had this to say about his approach to children: "I've always been myself. I never took a course in acting. I just figured that the best gift you could offer anybody is your honest self. . . ."[6]

~ 7 ~
Preparing the Message

CHILDREN'S SERMONS REQUIRE THE same careful preparation as sermons for adults, the same study, thought, and prayer—but with the children always in mind. We should not attempt too much in our talks with children. One clear point is enough, some important thought that might be conveyed in different ways, using an object or a story or a conversation.

Children's sermons force us to clarify and simplify what we want to say—a discipline that may also benefit us when we come to prepare our talks to adults. It is wise to write the talk out carefully to make sure the thinking is clear and the language is appropriate for children. But then the paper is best put away so we can speak directly to the children, face to face, person to person, soul to soul. As we speak, and especially if we have planned a conversation with the children, we may decide to depart from the remarks we have prepared, but even if we do, the preparation will help us express our thoughts more clearly.

We are preparing talks, not essays. We are trying to engage the children in what we are saying. One way to do that is to use personal pronouns such as "I," "you," and "we." Another way is to involve the children by asking them to use their imaginations: "Pretend that we are sitting in a boat with Jesus. It is a pretty day. The sun is shining, and the water is sparkling in the sunlight. And then the wind begins to blow, and the waves get bigger, and bigger. A storm is coming up." Still another way is to ask a question, "How would you feel if you were in that boat with Jesus when the storm came up?"

We can also suggest things for the children to think about. "Before you go to your seats, Jamie has something for you. Most of you know Jamie. She's been coming up here since she was only about as big as Antoine. Now she's starting sixth grade, and she's my helper today.

"What she has for you is a picture of Jesus in a boat. As you can see, it's a different kind of picture. You can only see Jesus from the back. It makes you think. It makes you ask yourself, What kind of person is Jesus? What kind of a person can say to a storm 'Stop!' and it stops?

"You can color the picture or hang it up in your room. Or you can show it to Mom or Dad or Grandma or Grandpa or all of them. Ask them what kind of person they think Jesus was. I'm going to keep one of the pictures in my study so I can think about that too."

As we write, we should be thinking of experiences from the children's lives that will help them understand us. Suppose we are writing about Daniel and the lion's den and we want to speak about our fears. We might say: "No, I don't think any of us will ever be put in a lion's den, but we do get into some pretty scary things, don't we? Maybe a tornado warning that sends us all to the basement. Maybe a trip to the hospital with everyone poking and jabbing us. Maybe some big kids at school giving us a hard time. And all the talk on television about bombs and wars. It's scary just to think about some of those things, isn't it?" Or if we are writing about the feeding of the five thousand, we might say, "I suppose the boy wanted to go see Jesus, and his mother said, 'All right, but you'd better let me make you a lunch.' And he probably said, 'Aw, Mom, I'll be the only kid there with a lunch.' But she made one anyway. They didn't have juice boxes or peanut butter and jelly, so she gave him five little loaves of bread made out of barley and two little fish for his lunch."

The beginning of the sermon is especially important. It is useful to begin with something in the children's experience, not only to get their attention, but because children learn new things, as we all do, by building on what they already know. That may be a toy or a game, but better yet it may be some emotion—fear or hope or joy or a sense of awe—or some event we have all experienced.

For many years, I served a church in a community where the making of maple syrup is a major industry, and where the Chamber of Commerce taps the trees in town. Each spring I would borrow a sap bucket from a tree near the church and talk to the children about the God who provides for us even through the trees around us. "There's a mystery in town," I would begin. "Someone has been hanging buckets on our trees, just like this bucket! Not on telephone poles, only on trees. You saw them too, didn't you? I wonder why they did that. Maybe we could ask Melissa's dad. He works with trees. Oh, I see Melissa's hand up. I think she knows."

As in any speech, transitions are essential. If I was talking before about a sap bucket and maple syrup, and I am now going to talk about the God who provides our food, how can I make sure the children follow me? A brief pause may be helpful, both to indicate a transition and to allow for a moment's reflection on what has already been said. Then perhaps a sentence or two to indicate that something new is coming. "If we can get such good things from a tree, I've been wondering how those good things got in the tree. How do you think they got there?" (My first inclination was to ask, "Who do you think put them there?" but that would have prompted the obvious answer, "God," perhaps without much thought. This question may too, but it may also prompt answers like "rain" or "sunshine" or "soil" that could provoke some more thought before leading back to God.)

One or two brief sentences may be all that is necessary for a good transition, yet these sentences need to be carefully prepared if the children are to follow us.

Conclusions are important, too, not only to emphasize the point of the sermon, but also to make sure that the children know the sermon is over and what they are to do next. "Right after church, I'm going to hang this bucket back on the tree I took it from. But it will be right across the street from the church, where I can look at it every day. When I see it, I'll remember the good things God gives us through trees. Maybe when you see a bucket you'll remember God's good gifts, too. Now let's say a prayer and thank God for trees and maple syrup—Jimmie says 'pancakes too!'; yes, we can thank God for pancakes, too—and then after our prayer you can go back to your seats."

If the sermon is concluded with prayer, thought should be given to it too. Is it a prayer *for* the children, asking God's blessing on them? Or is it a prayer *with* the children, putting into words the things they may not be able to verbalize themselves? There is a place for both kinds of prayer. In either case, the stereotyped language we so easily fall into when we pray—references to the "throne of grace," for example, or to "our sins of omission and commission"—may not be meaningful to the children. Even these brief prayers will be more useful if they are carefully prepared ahead of time.

At times, something is given to the children when they leave as a reminder of the sermon. If the gift relates directly to the sermon, it may serve a useful purpose. For example, if the story of Albrecht Dürer's *Praying Hands* were told,[1] a reproduction of the painting could become a cherished memento. Or if the children were introduced to Wilson Bentley and the "miracles of beauty" he discovered in snowflakes, reproductions of some of Bentley's photographs of snowflakes could provide the children with continuing wonderment.[2] Other meaningful gifts could encourage a response to a message: crayons and paper to draw a biblical picture; a litter bag to help clean up a neighborhood; a Christmas card to send to a shut-in, a teacher, or a sick classmate.

The children's sermon is one of the most important tasks of a pastor. There may be no one else in a child's life who talks about religion. There may be no one else who feels comfortable talking about spiritual things, or who will take the time, or who even cares about them. Immersed in the church, we can easily forget that some children live in families where religion is not discussed or may even be held in contempt. And yet, someone has brought the children to church, and they sit in the front of the church, looking up, expectantly. It is an opportunity, in the title of one of the better books on children's sermons, for "talking about something important" with the children.[3]

Still, serious as the talk may be, children must be dealt with gently. We should not load more on them than they can carry. They should not be given too many ideas to think about; they should not be made to feel too guilty or too responsible or too small. The twig can be bent in childhood, but we should be careful not to bend it too far. Children are vulnerable, like those biblical "bruised reeds" and "smoldering wicks."4 Some playfulness will help, as will humor, especially the kind that shows we don't take ourselves too seriously.

The humor will help us as well as the children. Halford Luccock wisely said once that "the amount of good a person can do depends greatly on how much fun he gets out of it."[5]

I have assumed that the pastor will be the one speaking to the children. I know that the task is sometimes given to someone else. That might be a Christian educator, a Sunday school teacher, a public school teacher, or even one of the church's young people. If the talk to the children is merely a lesson, some information to be learned, laypersons may be capable of doing a better job than the pastor. But if the talk is to be a sermon, drawn from scripture and spoken to the hearts of the children, someone theologically trained may be the better choice. Pastors who hesitate to undertake the task because they are unaccustomed to children can learn to speak to them—but then laypersons knowledgeable about the Bible but unaccustomed to preaching can also learn to prepare a sermon. The question in any situation is: Who is better able to speak God's Word to these children in ways that will reach both their minds and their hearts?

Those who present the Gospel to children are participating in a longer tradition than is commonly recognized. For centuries, preachers have spoken to children and experimented with how best to do it. Occasional sermons were preached to children in the Middle Ages, and during the Reformation they were often preached to children on Sunday afternoons. The pietists, and especially the Moravians, later revived the practice of sermons or talks to children.[6]

Children's sermons were published in America as early as 1739—when a Boston publisher printed a sermon preached to the children of the South Parish in Andover, Massachusetts—and collections of them began to appear in 1819. By the middle of the nineteenth century, separate worship services for children, with preaching, already common in England, were taking hold in the United States.[7]

About the same time, some ministers had adopted another practice: interrupting the morning sermon with a three- to four-minute digression directed specifically to the children. The typical five- to ten-minute sermon for children delivered in congregational worship in the way we are accustomed to today seems to have begun in both Great Britain and the United States in the 1870s.[8]

What is new today is that children's sermons are now widespread among many denominations and are accompanied by new expectations. Many congregations now expect that children's sermons will be included in worship and that they will be presented to the children with both thoughtfulness and skill. Those of us who speak to children need to be clear about the purpose of our messages and deliberate in our methods.

PART THREE: METHODS

~ 8 ~

The Setting

One of the difficulties of the children's sermon is the wide range of ages of the children who may be present. Older accounts speak of children as old as seventh graders being involved. That may be less common today, but even if the older children are in the fourth, fifth, or sixth grades, there is a great difference in understanding between them and the toddlers at their sides. If the children are of different ages, how does one address them?

My preference is to speak on the level of the older children who are present—not the very oldest, but the older ones. If one speaks always to the younger children, the older children will eventually stop coming, not wanting to be classed with the "babies." But if one speaks to the older children, the younger ones will still come, happy to be included, enjoying objects and stories and learning from the older children's comments and questions just as they do in many other situations. From time to time, the younger children can be specifically addressed, especially when the older ones can be enlisted to help with such things as teaching songs and responses, displaying objects, or distributing gifts, to acknowledge their growing maturity.

When we tell our congregations what our goals and expectations for the children's sermons are—as I think we should—we can let them know which children we expect to participate. If we would welcome even the youngest children, we can say just that, perhaps adding that parents are welcome to accompany their young children to the front of the church—or, as one pastor puts it, that the children are welcome to bring their parents forward with them, if they want to![1] If we are not comfortable speaking to children under a certain age, we can say that. Or if we want to include children older than those who usually participate, we can appeal to them for their participation, perhaps dropping the name "children's sermon" and making it clear that both "children" and "young people" are welcome to come forward. Those who are older may not want to be considered "children." As one of them told a pastor, "I don't think it should be called the children's sermon. The kids of the seventh and eighth grade are embarrassed to come down, but want to." Another added, "My sister is older too and wants to come down but she thinks she's too old when it is called a children's sermon."[2] Eventually, the older children will decide for themselves that they are too old to participate, but even then they, like the adults, will be listening to what is said.

What about the adults? They are present and listening. How should they be regarded? When I am speaking to children in a worship service, I am aware that others are listening, but I try to keep my attention solely on the children. This is their sermon, their opportunity to hear God's Word, and they deserve my full attention. Interrupting the talk with comments to the adults is seldom useful.

One of the few times it may be useful is when the adults are included in a conversation with the children. One person who spoke to children who were new to kindergarten asked the adults if any of them were starting something new and used their responses to show the children they were not alone in taking a new step in their lives, nor alone in being anxious about it.[3] It may also be useful to refer to the adults in our remarks to the children. I once talked to the children about nicknames, asking them to think of nicknames that would describe who they are now, who they would like to be, and who they thought God wants them to be. Then I said I would tell them a secret: "That's what all of us older people are doing here week after week, even those of us with gray hair, trying to see who we are and who we could be, and asking for help to become what God wants us to be." It is good for children to realize that things that are important in life cross all generations.

Whether adults are included in the sermon or not, they listen as the things they cherish are passed on to the children. They sometimes say they get more out of the children's sermons than the ones meant for adults. What they may be saying is that they have been able to hear our messages more clearly as we have simplified them for the children. Our sermons for adults are sometimes too complex, too abstract, too verbose, and the children's sermon may come as a welcome change. Or, as one of the early advocates of children's sermons put it, "Many older persons will have [in the children's sermon] five minutes of helpful service, instead of, to them, strange depths and heights and wanderings."[4] If adults are lost in the depths and heights and wanderings of the sermons meant for them, we may need to put greater effort into communicating with adults, while at the same time recognizing that a simple presentation of the Gospel in the children's sermon will also speak to many who are no longer children.

Another possibility is that the adults who say they like the children's sermons may be allowing themselves to hear the Gospel in a new way. When any of us are being "preached at," we may be on the defensive, holding what is said at arm's length. When, however, we overhear someone talk to children, our minds and hearts may be more open, allowing that which is childlike in us to listen with the children and hear what we have not heard before. Perhaps even without fully understanding what is happening, this indirect reception of the message may be what adults are describing.[5]

When adults listen to the children's sermon with the children, it creates the possibility of a dialogue between adults and children about the sermon during the week. Family members who might not otherwise speak to children about religious matters can see how such conversations are conducted and may feel free to talk to their children about the subject of last Sunday's children's sermon and how it relates to the children's lives and experiences. One pastor concludes his talk each week by telling the children to ask their parents or guardians about something they have heard.[6] Other pastors give parents suggestions for dialogues with their children about the children's sermon,[7] or gather groups of parents to discuss the effects of children's stories on their families.[8]

Children's sermons are sometimes misused by being subtly—or not so subtly—directed at the adults. A nineteenth-century Presbyterian pastor, J. L. McKee, writes unashamedly about aiming at the adults during his sermons to children: "It is very often the case that there is something you want to say to the grown people that is somehow at outs with the dignity, or propriety, or spirit of a sermon to them; but you can give them 'Hail, Columbia' over the heads of the children; and they can't say a word about it."[9]

Another minister inserted this note after one of his published sermons: "This sermon was preached to the children, with happy results, but it was intended for the parents—and it registered."[10] Whether done subtly or not, it is a mistake. The children's sermon is for the children, and they should not be abused by using their message as a pretext for aiming remarks at the adults.

Still, the adults present have every right to observe what is happening, to see any objects used with the children, and to hear what is said (which may mean repeating things children have said). And that raises the question of where the children should be during the sermon.

They are usually gathered at the front of the church to permit a more intimate presentation than if they stayed in their seats. Coming to the front also has the advantage of allowing the children to enter what may seem to them an especially holy part of the church, and that may be a meaningful experience in itself. At the front, they are sometimes seated on the chancel steps, facing the congregation. This allows the adults to see them, but it also means that the children are easily distracted by the congregation. Another disadvantage of that position is that ministers who sit on the steps with the children may find themselves unable to see all the children gathered around them and unable to speak to them face to face. Or if the ministers stand facing the children, they will be excluding the rest of the congregation by turning their backs on them.

In other churches, the children are seated on a front pew or on the floor facing the front of the church. In that case, the children are not distracted by the congregation and the minister can face both the children and the congregation, but the congregation is less able to observe the children as they interact with the minister.

An ideal setting would be one where the children and the minister are facing each other from different sides of the church. The children would not be distracted by looking at the congregation, but the congregation could still see them, and the minister could speak directly to them. But the church building itself will often dictate what arrangement is possible.

The position of the children's sermon in the order of service bears some thought. The children's sermon usually takes place early in the service. Then, when it is over, the children often leave the sanctuary. All this may occur before the scripture is read. But if the children's sermon is based on the scripture, it might be better to have it after the scripture is read. The children's sermon in that position would help everyone understand that the purpose of gathering the children is for them to be engaged by the Word of God.

Different services may suggest different places for the children's sermon. The children might be invited up and spoken to in relation to such things as communion, a baptism, a special offering, the introduction of advent candles or a crèche. Such talks are often merely educational, but they can be more than that if we speak to the ways these events matter to the children. If the children's sermon will come later than usual, let the children know that it will be coming; children are sometimes troubled if their routines are changed.

The length of the children's sermon is determined by two factors: the attention span of the children, and the time the congregation is willing to allow to the children. Older children can easily listen for five or ten minutes. Younger children may have difficulty paying attention that long. (The shortness of the attention span of young children, however, is sometimes over-emphasized; they are quite attentive to things that capture their interest. Try playing "which hand has the penny" with two-year-olds. You will tire of the game before they do.) One small survey indicated that churches devoted from three to fifteen minutes to children's sermons, with the largest group devoting five minutes.[11] Judging from book titles that include times in them, like *52 Three Minute Talks to Children* and *Three Hundred Five-Minute Sermons*, children's sermons usually last from two to six minutes.[12] Other book titles, however, make it appear that for some clergy the children's sermon is something to be rushed through and gotten over with: *Quick Children's Sermons*, *Children's Sermons to Go*, and *Snappy Sermonettes*.[13]

The time the congregation is willing to allow the children will also affect the frequency of children's sermons. If it is important to have children's sermons at all, I think it is important to have them every Sunday, although not every church does. Even churches that have a weekly children's sermon sometimes omit them on Sundays when "too much is happening"—communion, baptisms, new members, or stewardship campaigns. I wonder what that says to the children who have come to cherish "their time" in the service. "Their time" may, of course, be used for other kinds of presentations to them, a pageant for example, but ordinarily I would hope that the children's sermon would be among the last things to be sacrificed in order to save time.

~ 9 ~
Language

An 1885 essay on preaching to children began with a child's question, "'Papa,' said a preacher's little girl one Sunday morning, 'are you going to say anything today that I can understand?'"[1] Speaking to children in language they can understand has always been a challenge for adults. A frequent observation of children's sermons is that they are "over the children's heads." And with good reason. Here is a minister speaking to children about two officers of his church in a published sermon: "Mr. Cornwell acts as superintendent of the church school and correlates this important work, integrating the program and directing the efforts of a whole group of teachers. Mr. Anderson, as chairman of the ushers, has readied a group to assume duty in that capacity at services each week."[2]

Perhaps it didn't occur to the author of that sermon that few children are familiar with "correlating," "integrating," or "readying" anything in any "capacity."

A common recommendation given to those who speak to children is to "keep it simple." But what does that mean? It shouldn't mean talking down to them, keeping the ideas so simple that we risk insulting the children's intelligence; children can grasp deeper thoughts than we sometimes imagine. It is the language that needs to be simple. Children are still struggling with language. They say things like, "Tommy hitted the ball and I catched it." We may laugh and correct them but, more often than not, they are trying to speak correctly. In this case, a child applied a valid rule for the past tense without having learned yet that the rule has exceptions. Comprehending language presents similar challenges, such as deciphering new words, interpreting figures of speech, and distinguishing between things spoken seriously or humorously or tongue in cheek.

Helpful lessons on how to use language suitable for children can be found in the literature on readability.[3] The readability of a text is determined primarily by the length of the sentences and the difficulty of the words. The longer the sentences and the greater the number of difficult words, the more difficult the text will be for children. The grade level of a text can be determined by finding the average number of words and syllables in the sentences and then charting the numbers on a graph. The most widely used graph is included in Appendix A. Many word processing programs also do this.

Even though sermons are spoken rather than read—which makes them somewhat easier to understand—it is useful to consult a graph occasionally to check the sermons we have written for readability, comparing the results with the ages of the children to whom we usually speak. But even without a graph, it should be obvious that long, involved sentences, with subordinate clauses, parenthetical statements, clarifications and other digressions, and filled with polysyllabic words (like this sentence) will be hard for children to follow.

Look at the sentences you have written and see if they can be simplified. A sentence with a relative clause such as, "Peter, who was one of the twelve disciples, was also a fisherman," sounds like something written for adults. It can easily be simplified by dividing it into two sentences: "Peter was one of the twelve disciples. And he was a person who caught fish." A sentence that includes a parenthetical statement, like "Zacchaeus climbed up a tree (he had heard that Jesus was coming) so he could see Jesus better" can be simplified and made clearer at the same time. "When Zacchaeus heard that Jesus was coming, he climbed a tree. That way he could see Jesus better." Our sentences need not all be simple declarative sentences. More than one comma in a sentence, however, may indicate too much complexity. And in any case, the sentences should not be long.

Words with fewer syllables will usually be best, although there are exceptions. School children have already learned a good number of longer words, especially those associated with school: "mathematics," "multiplication," "cafeteria," "auditorium," "detention," "unexcused." Even pre-school children know a good many longer words: "hippopotamus," "television," "tricycle," "merry-go-round," "crybaby." On the other hand, some one-syllable words will be strange to all the children: "alb," "nave," "opt," "pyx," "scrim," "screed," "text."

The important thing with words is not so much how many syllables they contain but what words are within the children's experience. If you are unsure about a word, the best thing to do is to ask a child. (Writers often argue the case for including unfamiliar words to expand a child's understanding and vocabulary. That makes sense in written materials, where a child can stop and ponder the meaning of a word and let it play on the imagination. It makes less sense when we are talking to children and our chief object is to be understood—unless we are willing to stop and explain what a new word means.)

The use of familiar, shorter words should not be confused with "baby talk," the use of childish words and imperfect grammar that is rightly resented by children. Baby talk is condescending; it doesn't take the growing abilities of children seriously. Shorter words in themselves, however, will not be resented. If well chosen, they have power—even with adults—to convey meaningful and memorable thoughts. Consider the last two lines of one of Shakespeare's sonnets:

> So long as man can breathe, or eyes can see,
> So long lives this, and this gives life to thee.[4]

Or this little poem by Emily Dickinson:

> A word is dead
> When it is said,

Some say.
I say it just
Begins to live
That day.[5]

In general, use concrete words—"grass," "bread," "basket"—rather than abstract words—"vegetation," "nourishment," "container"—which are more difficult for children. Children quickly learn some abstractions—that the word "dog," for example, applies to animals as diverse as Chihuahuas and Great Danes, but even a child who knows a good deal about dogs will not learn much from a discussion of "the essentials of canine nutrition."

Be wary of any word that ends in "tion," as well as words that end in "ance," "ary," "ence," "ism," "ity," "ment," "ness," "ology," "ous," "sion," and "tics" (although children will know some of them, such as "basement," "delicious," and "vacation"). Prefixes are also often signs of difficult words: "dis," "ex," "extra," "multi," "non," "post," "pre," "pro," "semi," "sub," and "un." But again, schoolchildren will know some of them, such as "multiplication" and "substitute."

Even concrete words, however, may be outside children's experience. Words such as "cowcatcher," "finial," "keystone," "micrometer," and "pig iron" are concrete but will probably not be understood.

Often words that are outside children's experience can easily be replaced with more familiar words. Just as we say "eye doctor" instead of "ophthalmologist," we can substitute "song" for "anthem," "reading stand" for "lectern," and "cup" for "chalice."

We should be cautious with figurative language. Children may see only the concrete meaning of terms such as "God's mighty hand" or "taking up your cross" and misunderstand what we are saying, and they may have no idea what we mean if we refer to God as "our rock." Children take things literally. I remember being disappointed the first time I crossed a state line; I had expected to see a line somewhere.

Pronouns are another source of confusion. Consider the statement: "Judas came with some soldiers to the garden where Jesus was praying. Then he kissed him." Of course, we know who kissed whom, but the children may not. Unless it is absolutely clear to whom a pronoun refers, use the name or the noun again.

Words of obligation—"should," "ought to," "have to," "must"—are best used sparingly. If we can persuade children to do something rather than tell them that they *must* do it, there is a better chance that it will be done. Children, like adults, resent being told to do something and may resist doing it.

When children seem not to understand something, it may be only the word we have used that they don't understand; the concept may be fully understood. Children all understand "being fair" ("No fair!" they say) though they may not be familiar with the word "justice." They can understand as well as an adult can when we say that "God is everywhere, knows everything, and can do anything," although the words "omnipresent," "omniscient," and "omnipotent" will be strange to them.

Like those three words, much of the religious language we regularly use is too abstract for children. A kindergarten teacher paused while reading a story to ask her students if they knew what the phrase "people are not grateful" meant. One girl decided that it meant "people are not great." A boy suggested tentatively "don't eat grapefruit?"[6] Children who don't understand "grateful" will certainly not understand "righteousness," "salvation," "liturgy," "intercession," "covenant," or "sin." We may choose to teach them the meaning of a new word like "sin," or we may be able to use simpler terms in its place, for example "doing wrong" or "disappointing God," or we may decide that the children are not yet ready for either the word or the concept.

Even a simple word like "faith" may not mean much to children in the abstract. We can make it meaningful, however, by embodying it in a specific event or person. They will understand what an exciting and unsettling venture it was when Abraham trusted God and set out for a land he had never seen, and when they do, we can give the name "faith" to that experience. Examples from children's lives and experiences will be especially helpful in making abstract concepts meaningful. Something I saw in school, for example, was useful in explaining kindness: "Kind people look for someone who needs a friend. I saw a little kindergarten boy crying in school one day. A girl was sitting beside him. She was a little older, and when she saw he was crying she reached out and held his hand. She was being kind to him."

Poetry communicates as much through feeling as through thought, and it matters less whether all the words in a poem are understood. Joyce Kilmer's "Trees" contains at least two difficult words, "bosom" and "intimately." But in the main it will be understood and, because of its beauty, it will be appreciated and remembered.

When we talk to children, we need to choose our words carefully. I was once given a beautiful chambered nautilus, and I couldn't wait to show it to the children. I read the last verse of Oliver Wendell Holmes's poem "The Chambered Nautilus" to them and gave them copies of it. Looking back, I realize that that verse's first line alone, "Build thee more stately mansions, O my soul," contains two two-syllable words that would be difficult for many children: "stately" and "mansions." But in addition to that, three of the one-syllable words are also difficult: the archaic "thee," the vocative "O," and the elusive "soul." I am not sure now that that line meant anything to the children. I have since learned to be more careful with language.

Despite all our efforts, children may misunderstand the words we use. When Elizabeth Peabody was a child, her mother told her about her Pilgrim ancestors. Young Elizabeth pictured them as "a procession of fair women in white robes as sisters . . ., who strangely enough were all named Ann."[7] Words that can have more than one meaning are especially ripe for misunderstanding. Our granddaughter Louisa, when she was young, was playing with some envelopes, carrying them to the mail slot in the front door. When asked what she was doing with them, she said, "I'm delivering them from evil."

Still, as difficult as words can be, children are fascinated by them and will gladly join you in word play: tongue twisters: ("I saw Esau kissing Kate, / The fact is we all three saw; / For I saw him, / And he saw me, / And she saw I saw Esau");[8] riddles ("What kind of lights did Noah use on the ark? Floodlights"); conundrums ("blackberries are red when they're green"); gigantic words ("supercalifragilisticexpialidocious," "antidisestablishmentarianism"); funny words ("fiddle-faddle," "fiddledeedee," "fiddlesticks"); and funny names (Rancid W. Veeblefester, Olive Oyl). Take time to enjoy the language with them.

That enjoyment will help create an appropriate tone for speaking to children. They expect us to speak to them as adults, providing insights they cannot provide for themselves, but adult formality and austerity may create an unhelpful barrier between us and them. The children will appreciate our stepping away from the pulpit, literally and figuratively, and taking time to enjoy language and life with them.

Inclusive language can easily be used with children. Some adults resist it, saying that they have learned to see "him" and "man" as inclusive and don't see the necessity for change. But children have a different perspective. They will assume that "him" and "man" refer to males. One need not make an issue of inclusive language, cluttering sermons with the repeated use of "her or his." Usually all that is needed is to recast our sentences in the plural, for example, changing "each child brought his Bible" (or "her or his Bible") to "the children brought their Bibles." Or the pronouns can often simply be omitted: "each child brought a Bible."

Inclusive language involves more than pronouns. We should be fair to both girls and boys in everything we say. All our references should not be to dolls on the one hand or football on the other but to both kinds of activities or, better yet, to activities cherished by both girls and boys.

Inclusive language can also be used with reference to God. God is, after all, neither male nor female, and our language should help children understand that (which will answer the question "Is there a Mrs. God?" even before it is asked). Eliminating the traditional masculine references to God sometimes results in clumsy language like "God will reveal God's ways in God's own time," but it doesn't have to.

Christians have referred to God in many ways, and we can use those different names when we speak with children. We have all sung:

> Thy mercies how tender, how firm to the end,
> Our Maker, Defender, Redeemer, and Friend![9]

The list of divine names goes on: Counselor, Creator, Deliverer, the Eternal, Giver, Guide, the Holy One, the Living God, the Mighty One, the Most High, Protector, Savior, Shepherd, our Strength. In Brian Wren's words, we can "Bring Many Names"[10] into our sermons, and in doing so enrich the children's understanding of God.

There is another issue of inclusiveness. Often we address the children as "you," and that is sometimes appropriate as in "what you do in school." But it is good to put ourselves in their company by saying "we" as often as possible: "We make mistakes, don't we?" We can also reach out to children by using the words "I" and "me." We sometimes use the language of the classroom, where the teacher will refer to herself in the third person, saying things like "Mrs. Wilson had better not see you looking at anyone else's paper." Mrs. Wilson is properly asserting her authority in that way, but it is not useful for us to refer to ourselves by saying things like "Pastor Bob is glad to see you this morning" or "Your pastor prays for you every day." A simple "I" or "me" breaks down the barriers that age, size, and clerical garb too often create.

We should also bear in mind that we are not addressing "children" in general but the individuals seated in front of us. Clarence Day never felt at ease with his pastor, the Reverend Doctor Owen Lloyd Garden. He writes that Garden "never seemed to speak to me personally, but to a thing called My Child. He was more at home speaking to a large audience than to a small boy. . . ."[11] "My Child" isn't heard much anymore, but Day might have had the same feeling about pastors who speak to "you children" or "you youngsters" or "my little friends" rather than to Damon and Patty and Dorie and the other individuals gathered around them.

If you really want to communicate with children, ask some knowledgeable adult—an elementary school teacher, for example—to listen to your sermons and to tell you when and how you are talking down to the children or talking over their heads. Perhaps at the same time this person can call your attention to the infelicities and mistakes we all make in public speaking, but that few people have the kindness to tell us about.

~ 10 ~
Objects

PERHAPS THE MOST COMMON CHILDREN'S sermon is one that involves an object. The titles of many collections of children's sermons show the frequency of the approach: *Children's Object Sermons for the Seasons*; *Promises and Turtle Shells: and 49 Other Object Lessons for Children*; *Junior Surprise Sermons with Hand-made Objects*; *Object Lessons with Easy to Find Objects*; and on and on.[1] One author advises preachers to "find a prop, a trick, or a game that conveys the thought, or even carries the burden of the message."[2] The advantage of an object is obvious: sight as well as sound, and perhaps touch or taste or smell as well, are engaged and, when an everyday object is used, encountering it later will recall and reemphasize its message.

The use of an object for instructing children has a long history, going back at least to the late eighteenth century and Johann Heinrich Pestalozzi's belief that learning should start with material objects rather than abstract concepts. Ironically, the use of objects in children's sermons is often criticized today because the objects are being used as a way of introducing abstractions—such as loyalty, kindness, mercy, and faith—too difficult for children to understand.

The criticisms are often valid. One minister used an apple and a bowl when speaking about faith. He put the apple on a table and covered it with the bowl and explained to the children that it was faith that let them believe the apple was still there even though they could no longer see it. At the end, he asked the children: "What is faith?" and one boy answered: "an apple under a bowl."[3]

Another minister also uses apples as objects. He suggests filling a small barrel with apples and placing one rotten apple in the middle of the barrel. Then the children can be told how one rotten apple can spoil a whole barrel and how in the same way one bad thought can spoil our good thoughts. At the end of the talk, the children are to be sent back to their pews with apples from the barrel as reminders of the lesson.[4] The difficulty with the lesson is twofold. First, it may be hard for children to understand how one apple can spoil the others. But even if that is understood, the children may not follow the leap from the concrete spoiling of apples to the abstract spoiling of ideas. A younger child, especially, may go home with an apple and nothing more. (An older child may wonder whether the apple should be eaten; didn't the minister say that one rotten apple in the barrel will spoil all the rest?)

Like the potentially-spoiled apples given as gifts, objects are sometimes presented in confusing ways. For a sermon on the text "You are the salt of the earth," one author suggests that we fill two glasses, one with plain water and one with salt water. Then we are to have the children taste them to see if they can tell the difference. The exercise is to show them that salt changes things.[5] Indeed it does, but in this case the salt changes the taste of the water for the worse. Is that what Christians are to do for the world?

Still other suggested uses of objects are too often simply inept:

> Have a roll of paper stuck in your ear. Unroll the paper to show sins that keep us from hearing God's voice. . . . Pull a puppet's skirt over its head and say, 'A person wrapped up in himself makes a small package.' . . . Show [a] puppet soaring on a Bible equipped with paper wings to depict the life of one who lives by God's word.[6]

But even though objects can be used inappropriately or confusingly or ineptly, they are often helpful. Every child will recognize a chalkboard and will understand what we are doing when we write something on it and then erase it. We can ask the child to imagine that the wrong things we have done are all written on the chalkboard but that God is willing to erase them and forget them. I think the mental picture of our sins on a chalkboard and God erasing them is a legitimate use of an object. It does not explain the abstract concept of forgiveness but rather gives one concrete way of understanding the concept.

Geodes are also useful objects. Geodes appear to be common rocks, but they are hollow, and the cavity is usually lined with crystals. When cut in half and polished, they are strikingly beautiful inside, despite a plain looking exterior. Geodes are a useful way to demonstrate the idea that appearances can be deceiving, and that we should not judge by them. And that, in turn, may help children understand us when we say that God does not judge by appearances.

Objects, used carefully, have a place in children's sermons. Too often we talk in generalities only, while children are used to dealing with things that are concrete. They use their fingers to learn mathematics; they are taught about fractions with pictures of pies and about centrifugal force by swinging a bucket of water. Wise teachers have always done what Shakespeare describes as giving "airy nothing a local habitation and a name."[7]

Children think concretely, which can be seen in their prayers. A child's prayer from Indonesia included this petition: "Bless us all, including the little brown and white dog that came and stayed with us."[8] A little girl offered a prayer before the refreshment break in Vacation Bible School: "Lord, we thank you for the many Popsicles, and especially that we've had a different color each day."[9] A child whose grandmother had undergone abdominal surgery prayed at her bedside: "Please take care of Grandma 'cause she has strings holding her tummy together."[10]

Hans Christian Andersen understood how children think. In one of his stories the Snow Queen promises to give a boy the whole world—and a new pair of skates. The whole world may not mean much to a boy, but a new pair of skates is sure to capture his interest.[11]

Objects—like those new skates—are useful in speaking to children, and their usefulness goes beyond explaining abstract concepts. An object may be used in a children's sermon simply to arouse interest. In the sermons in Jerry Jordan's books, some object is brought each week hidden in a brown paper bag. The bag itself arouses interest even before the object in it is revealed, and provides continuity and expectation from week to week.[12] Puppets, too, create interest, even before they say a word.

Objects can also be used as illustrations. If something in a story is unfamiliar to the children, it might help them to see the object in question. A shepherd's crook, a sling, or a model of a Near Eastern house can help illustrate a biblical story in the same way that pictures are used in a book.

The object may, of course, be itself the thing that will be talked about—the Bible, for example. Different kinds of Bibles could be brought to make a discussion of the Bible more vivid: new and old Bibles, large and small ones, Bibles in Braille and in other languages. Surely, someone in the congregation could read a passage from a Bible in a different language, which would be an object lesson in itself. If the minister includes a Bible that has a special, personal meaning—one received as a child, for example, with a childish signature—the Bible may help to form a bond between the children and a person they can now think of as having once been a child too.

Works of religious art—paintings, poetry, and music—are objects that can bring children into God's presence in an immediate and compelling way. The great painters have portrayed much of scripture, and the best poets and composers have put the faith in word and song. We can show the children Rembrandt's *Head of Christ* or Georges Rouault's *Christ Mocked by Soldiers* (if we explain that those artists were trying to show the kind of person Jesus was rather than what he looked like). We can read to them from James Weldon Johnson's *God's Trombones* or let them listen to a selection from Handel's *Messiah*. How much better to let the children see and hear art of that quality than to settle for the latest offerings of the religious book stores!

Some of the best objects for children's sermons are found in the world around us, natural objects that elicit awe and wonder and mystery, not illustrating or symbolizing anything but revealing something about God through the world God made. The Psalmist heard God speaking in nature: "The heavens are telling the glory of God; and the firmament proclaims [God's] handiwork" (Ps. 19:1). And in the same way the Apostle Paul saw the Creator revealed in the world around him: "Ever since the creation of the world [God's] eternal power and divine nature, invisible though they are, have been understood and seen through the things [God] has made" (Rom. 1:20). Natural objects will not tell us all that revelation tells us about God, but they can be used to give children vivid glimpses of the Creator.

Those objects can be anything in nature: buds in spring, flowers in summer, leaves in the fall, snowflakes in winter. "Earth's crammed with heaven," Elizabeth Barrett Browning says, "And every common bush afire with God."[13]

Albert Einstein was profoundly influenced by the wonder of a compass he was given when he was five years old.[14] Walt Whitman found "full starr'd nights" "give hints to the soul, impossible to put in a statement." One summer, contemplating another natural object—the mullein, a common weed—he was convinced that "every object has its lesson."[15]

William Blake found those lessons in a grain of sand and a wild flower:

> To see a World in a Grain of Sand
> And a Heaven in a Wild Flower
> Hold Infinity in the palm of your hand
> And Eternity in an hour.[16]

Alfred, Lord Tennyson pondered a "flower in the crannied wall" and thought that if he could understand

> What you are, root and all, and all in all,
> I should know what God and man is.[17]

Scientists, too, have seen something of God in the objects of nature. George Washington Carver once said that, to him, "nature in its varied forms are the little windows through which God permits me to commune with him, and to see much of his glory, by simply lifting the curtain, and looking in."[18] Even if we are not scientists, we may be able to help lift the curtain so some child can look in.

Another scientist, Rachel Carson, shows in her little book The Sense of Wonder how that can be done. She simply shares natural marvels with children, with no concern for scientific names or explanations. It is enough, she says, to allow children to see what we have found to be "beautiful and awe-inspiring," to "drink in the beauty, and think and wonder at the meaning" of the world around us.[19]

To put it more vividly, our task is to do for children what Emily Dickinson's father, Edward Dickinson, did for the village of Amherst, Massachusetts, when he ran out and violently rang the church bell one evening to call the villagers' attention to a sky that was "a beautiful red, bordering on a crimson," with "rays of a gold pink color" shooting off from the center.[20]

When children are gathered in worship and we call their attention to some wonder of nature—cherry blossoms, for example, or a kitten or amethyst crystals or maple seeds that come helicoptering down through the air—it may not be necessary to say anything further. In fact, it may be wise not to interrupt the children's awe at God's handiwork. Or we may find it useful to help them think about what they are experiencing, probing with our questions to help them see the Creator behind the creation, or helping them to offer their gratitude to the Creator in prayer, or perhaps merely making a quiet statement such as "Isn't God amazing!" to set the tone for some silent meditation.

God's wonders presented in worship may profoundly affect a child. Barbara Brown Taylor's minister once talked about her in his sermon—"a little girl who kept tadpoles in a birdbath so that she could watch over them as they turned into frogs"—and compared her care for the tadpoles to God's care for all creation. To think about a tadpole connecting her life to God changed the way she saw the world. "When the service was over that day," she said, "I walked out of it into a God-enchanted world, where I could not wait to find further clues to heaven on earth. Every leaf, every ant, every shiny rock called out to me—begging to be watched, to be listened to, to be handled and examined. I became a detective of divinity, collecting evidence of God's genius and admiring the tracks left for me to follow."[21]

Too often, instead of natural wonders, children's sermons exhibit toys and gimmicks that elicit little awe or wonder and reveal little about the Creator. An internet site advertised a "Ready-to-Do Children's Message Kit" with twenty-four children's messages and "9 fun gizmos." "Gizmos in each box will be: 5 Brite-Tites, 20 linking stars, 1 sticky hand, 1 inflatable heart, 1 foam brick, 1 horseshoe magnet, 1 bag of shiny ribbons, 1 crazy bouncer, and 20 plastic coins"[22]

In a way, God is one of those unseen things so difficult for children to understand, and our challenge is to find ways to make God tangible and real. But, of course, at the heart of the Christian message is the incarnation; Jesus is for us the one in whom we see God. Jesus is "the image of the invisible God" (Col. 1:15). We have the great privilege by our preaching to introduce the children to Jesus, to bring them into his presence, and in that way to bring them into the presence of God. And for that reason, if we use the lectionary, the Gospel lessons will more often than not provide the texts for our sermons.

In a lesser way, many of the Christian virtues are incarnated in people. Why not introduce the children to some of them? Wonder can be seen in a newborn child, love in the parents of an adopted child, devotion in a newly-ordained minister, faithfulness in a couple celebrating a golden anniversary, self-sacrifice in a local hero, service in young people going to a work camp—perhaps even redemption in someone returning to the church from prison. What better living objects to bring before the children?

And then there is that great cloud of witnesses from the past to whom we could introduce the children, relating incidents from the lives of people such as St. Francis, Fanny Crosby, Father Damien, George Washington Carver, Albert Schweitzer, and Mother Theresa. In them and people like them the Christian faith is wonderfully objectified.

Often, when an object is used, it is introduced first with the question: "Can anyone tell me what this is?" That puts the focus on the object. It may be more useful to begin with the theme of the talk and then to introduce an object to illustrate the theme. That puts the focus on the theme, where it belongs. And that may be the better way to prepare for any object sermon: to decide what we want to say and then to search through our experience to find an object that will help us say it.

Sometimes, however, the sermon comes to mind the other way around: we meet some object that calls out for a sermon. Henry Sloane Coffin was once quarantined on a Japanese ship, and the only book in English he could find to read was a copy of the International Marine Signal Code. With the book's help, he learned to identify the signal flags on ships entering the harbor. One he saw frequently read: "I need a pilot." A copy of that flag was soon run up beside his pulpit for a children's sermon.[23]

On a visit to the Oregon coast, I saw a seal pup all alone on the beach. It would scoot up to passersby and look at them with its big eyes as if to ask: "Are you my mother?" A gathering crowd became worried about the pup there by itself and called a ranger, but when he came he said that we didn't need to worry about it. Baby seals don't swim well, so the mothers leave them on the beach to rest and then come back to nurse them. The pup's mother hadn't forgotten it and would soon be back for it. I found a stuffed seal in a store, bought it, and used it the next Sunday to tell the children about the lonely seal pup and its unseen but nurturing mother—so much like another unseen, nurturing presence.

One use of objects seems questionable to me, that of the "mystery box." R. Douglas Reinard asked a different child each week to bring some item that would be hidden in a shoebox until the time for the children's sermon. Only when the children gathered, would he take it out, learn what it was, and say something about it.[24] In a variation on Reinard's plan, anyone in the congregation can volunteer to provide the mystery item. In both cases, the children and the congregation are always eager to see what the item will be and what the minister will say about it. Nevertheless, either plan seems to me to have several flaws.

First, it allows others to choose the subjects for the sermons, which results in a randomness to the presentations that is in sharp contrast to sermons that follow the lectionary or some other planned approach. And the objects themselves may have little relationship to the Christian message. Objects as varied as a cracked golf ball, a lottery ticket, or a bottle of nail polish may appear, which are hardly prime materials for a children's sermon.

Second, the approach does not give the minister time to prepare. How much better it would be if time were given to prepare a sermon with consideration for both the children's needs and their capabilities!

Third, the approach can easily degenerate into a game of "let's stump the preacher" among those who bring the objects. A clever preacher can always find something to say about any object, but it will be the cleverness—or confusion—of the minister that most people will remember rather than what was said.

The use of magic in children's sermons is also questionable. Magic tricks are sure to hold the children's attention, but younger children may think what is done is magic and misunderstand the message. The older children have learned that magic tricks are always just that—tricks, some form of deceit—which creates the possibility that using magic will somehow convey to those children that God acts by deceit, that religion is a trick which can be explained away. In the collection Children's Letters to God, one girl asks God: "Are you really invisible or is that just a trick?"[25]

There is a danger that the presentation of objects will degenerate into showmanship, blurring the line between worship and entertainment. If ministers are seen putting bananas in their ears or showing how to make a pickle glow in the dark or a soda can crush itself (yes, those are real examples),[26] and especially if more time is devoted to those actions than to the message itself, will the message be remembered? No harm can be found in entertaining objects if they enhance the message, but sometimes they overshadow it.

I think the careful use of objects can be helpful in communicating with children, but the mere fact of including an object in a children's sermon does not guarantee that the children will learn anything. James Whitcomb Riley amused his contemporaries with a parody of an object lesson in which he described an educator who used a peanut to speak to a group of primary children. During his brief talk, the educator managed to speak over the children's heads, make light of their responses, and hold up to ridicule the answer he said "a stupid little boy" had given him on another occasion—while never reaching any conclusions about the peanut. I have included Riley's sketch in Appendix B as a cautionary object lesson about object lessons.

~ 11 ~
Analogies

OFTEN THE USE OF OBJECTS DEPENDS on an analogy. We show the children a penny, for example, and tell them that the way a penny is stamped with Lincoln's image is like the way we are stamped with God's image. The use of analogies with children, however, is much broader than that. Analogies are one of the best ways we have of helping children learn. Something that is already understood is used to explain something that is not yet understood. The new thing, we say, is like this other, familiar thing. God is like a good parent. Prayer is like talking on a telephone to someone we can't see. Forgiveness is like God erasing our sins.

Learning by analogy is one of the chief ways we all learn. Sound waves, we are taught, are like the ripples that go out in a pond when we throw a stone in the water. The mind is like an iceberg, partly visible to us in the conscious mind but mostly hidden in the unconscious. We often argue from analogies, as a generation of political leaders did when they warned us that if communism were not checked, countries would fall to it "like dominoes."

Analogies are a useful tool in preaching to children as they are in teaching them, but they have an obvious weakness. However striking the commonalities between two items, some difference always exists, and that difference may be significant. When we talk to someone on a telephone, there is a line or a cell tower to make the connection.

Heaven has no cell towers or telephone lines to connect us to God. And such a difference calls the whole comparison in question.

Arguments from analogy are also flawed. The domino theory is impressive until one realizes that countries are not objects that can be stood up and then toppled like a row of dominoes but are comprised of people who make choices of their own. There is, strictly speaking, no valid argument from analogy, for one can always respond, "Yes, there are those similarities, but what about these differences?"

What an analogy can do, however, is to suggest a new way of thinking about something. If on Easter we show the children candles that always light themselves when we try to blow them out, that doesn't prove anything about the resurrection, but it suggests that amazing things happen in this world and we shouldn't too easily say that something can't happen. If we say that God is like the air, which we can breathe and feel but can't see, we haven't proved that God exists, but we have suggested that things that are invisible can still be real. Without proving anything, analogies can suggest things that might be true and new ways of thinking about things that we already believe to be true.

When we use analogies with children, we need to be honest with them about the differences between the things we are comparing. Yes, God is like a parent in many ways, and that is a useful analogy, but we need to make sure the children understand that God is not indulgent like some parents or unfeeling and abusive like others. The more perceptive children will already have noted some of the differences, and we need to assure them that we are aware of them too. The other children also need to know the differences so they don't misunderstand what we are saying.

Jerry Jordan was careful to do this when he showed the children a magnet and said that its "pulling power" made him think of God. To make sure the children didn't misunderstand him, he added: "Just so you don't get a mistaken idea, or think I'm funny, no, I'm not saying God either looks like this big magnet or works the same way. That would be foolish. What makes me think of God, however, is that we are always being pulled, or drawn, toward God."[1]

One way to use analogies honestly is to avoid saying that one thing is "like" another and simply saying that something "reminds me" or "makes me think" of something else.[2] "The way a hen gathers her chicks under her wings to protect them reminds me of the way God protects us when we are in trouble" is much better than saying "God is like a hen" with the strange picture that might bring to a child's mind. That kind of statement avoids any thought about how similar or different two things are and says merely that they suggest a way of thinking to you and that they may be suggestive to the children as well.

An analogy will succeed only if the children can see the connection between the two things we are comparing. One author of children's sermons suggests that the children be given brooms, rags, and feather dusters for an Advent children's sermon and that they be asked to sweep and dust the church as a way of preparing for Christ's coming.[3] I assume that the housecleaning is meant to represent some deeper, spiritual preparation for Christ's coming, but apart from a brief mention in the concluding prayer that is never said. Without an explicit reference to spiritual preparation, will the children understand that Advent has any purpose other than cleaning the church? (The connection could easily be made by referring to such spiritual housecleaning as "throwing out our bad habits, shining up our good habits, sweeping out the mean and selfish things we do, and making room for Jesus.")

Some of our analogies are unsuccessful because they are not really analogies but only words used in different ways. One minister showed the children a banana peel and talked about slipping on it. Then he compared that with a slip of the tongue.[4] Another minister showed the children a wristwatch and went on to tell them about a whale watch. On another occasion he showed them "holey things"—a doughnut, a pair of pants with several holes—and used them to talk about what makes our faith "holy and pleasing to God."[5] An author suggests showing the children a ruler and then talking to them about rules.[6] I find these plays on words confusing; I wonder what children make of them.

A good analogy, on the other hand, can be very persuasive. In one of his published sermons, Harold Steindam shows a wilted plant to the children and then explains how he had heard about talking to plants and so tried to make it healthy by talking to it, without success. The children realize that it needs more than talk; he has to give it water. He agrees and has them water it, and then he says: "People are like this too. It's nice to say kind words to someone, but sometimes kind words alone aren't enough. Sometimes we have to *do* something to help, just as we had to give some water to our plant, and not just talk to it." And then he gives examples of the kind things children can do for others. The analogy is close and clearly stated and should be meaningful to children.[7]

I have learned to be cautious with analogies, but I still use them. I like to tell the children how I enjoy feeding birds. "We have five different bird feeders in our yard, and I love to feed the birds. They come and eat, and then they fly away, and they don't even say 'thank you.' But I don't care. I just like to see them eat and hear them sing. I don't like it when they fight over the seeds, but I still feed them whether they fight or not.

"Feeding the birds always makes me think of God. God puts out food for the birds, too, seeds and worms and bugs. And God puts out food for us: apples, strawberries, brussel sprouts (what? you don't like brussel sprouts?)—well, how about oranges or corn on the cob? God gives us all this good food, and sometimes we don't say 'thank you' either. I think God would like us to say 'thank you,' but even if we don't the food is still there for us. And God is disappointed when we fight over who got the most strawberries, but even when we do, the berries keep growing. God is amazing! And God never forgets our food. I forget to feed the birds sometimes, but God doesn't forget. Isn't God amazing? This week, when you see birds eating their food, think how God feeds us—and maybe say the little 'thank you' that we sometimes forget to say."

Another Sunday I took a trash bag and filled it with trash lying along the street next to the high school. Then I took it with me to talk to the children. "Does anyone here like to draw or paint? Suppose you made a pretty picture at school and took a lot of time to get it just right. And then someone came along and poured ketchup on it or tore it or stepped on it with muddy boots. How would you feel?

"I think God is an artist too. God made this pretty world and took the time to get it just right. Just think of the beautiful things God put in the world: the blue sky and green grass and daffodils and snowflakes and clouds and squirrels and honking geese flying in a V and deer in the woods. God made this pretty world, and then people spoil it. Look what I found along the street by the high school. I wonder how God feels when people throw things along the street like that." (When I had finished all that I had to say, I gave each child a grocery bag and asked them to help me clean up God's world.)

Analogies are one of our best tools, if used honestly and carefully.

~ 12 ~
Stories

STORIES AND CHILDREN'S SERMONS are well-matched. The message we have for children comes to us as story in the scriptures. Even though the overarching biblical story—of God's redemption of sinful humanity—may be beyond children's comprehension, individual stories within it are well suited to children.

But not all of them. Some biblical stories are clearly not meant for children. Consider, for example, the stories of Amnon's rape of Tamar or of Samuel's hewing Agag to pieces. The Bible contains other violent stories, and we may differ in which ones we think suitable for children. The story of David and Goliath with its message of God's empowerment has always been a favorite, but I find it hard to commend young David, standing before Saul with Goliath's large and bloody head in his hand, to the young children gathered in the front of the church. And I am uneasy with one author's suggestion of a children's sermon about the death of John the Baptist. The author tells how John's head was given to Herodias's daughter on a platter without making any comment on the violence except the casual remark: "I'll bet she wished she'd asked for a necklace, don't you?"[1] I am not convinced that bloody heads go well with children's sermons, but if they are included, the children deserve to be given some perspective on the violence. This is what I have said after telling the story of David and Goliath.

"There's something about that story I like and something I don't like. I don't like the part about killing Goliath. I wish David had been a cowboy and could have lassoed Goliath, or a park ranger and could have tranquilized him—given him a shot to make him go to sleep—as they do with wild animals. But some bad things happen in this world—even killing—and when the Bible tells stories it includes those things too.

"What I like about the story is how sure David was that God would help him, even against a giant. It's good to know that God is there to help us. We don't have to fight giants, but sometimes we have things in our lives that seem like giants: subjects in school we don't understand; bullies on the playground; unhappy things at home. But like David, we can say 'I can't handle this by myself, but with God's help, I can.' And God is always there to help us."

The story of Abraham and Isaac on Mount Moriah is another difficult story. I find it deeply meaningful. Kierkegaard's probing thoughts about it in his *Fear and Trembling*, read years ago, still affect my thinking.[2] But even though the story includes a child, it is not a story for children. What will children make of Abraham's willingness to kill his own son? If fathers can think of killing their sons, what doubts might that raise in the children's minds about their fathers? And if God commanded Abraham to kill Isaac, what is God really like? The story can be bewildering to a child.[3] Even the story of Noah's ark, with all those beloved animals, is a darker story than we might want to tell children. One six-year-old responded to the story by saying how dreadful it must have been for Noah to see all those dead bodies when he came out of the ark.[4] If we tell these stories, our presentation of them needs to be thought through carefully.

Many of the biblical stories, however, are stories we can gladly share with children: stories that convey religious truths in a way that talks and lessons cannot; stories in which abstract words like "faith" and "love" become flesh in the characters portrayed; stories that speak to deep, hidden places in our souls. Some of those stories can be told very much as they are in the Bible. Who could improve on the parables of the Prodigal Son or the Good Samaritan? They can be read or told to the children or they could be acted out for the children—or even by the children. They could also be told in a modern setting to help bring the message home.

Biblical stories can be adapted for different ages. God's call to Samuel, for example, is well suited for responses by younger children. They can be taught to call out "Here I am, for you called me" at the appropriate times in the story. A painting like Sir Joshua Reynolds's "The Young Samuel" could be shown to help children imagine what Samuel might have looked like.

Stories can be combined with songs. Children can be taught to sing "Go Down, Moses" as they learn about the Exodus.[5] As they learn about Jacob's dream at Bethel, they can learn to sing "We Are Climbing Jacob's Ladder." That song, in turn, could lead to another story, especially for older children: the story of the freed American slaves and the inspiration they received and gave to others by singing "We Are Climbing Jacob's Ladder."

Often biblical stories can be brought to life through modern parallels. The parable of the mustard seed is well illustrated by the story of Rosa Parks's unwillingness to move to the back of the bus. That act of a woman tired from work and tired of second-class citizenship was the smallest of protests, but the protest grew and grew until today we have to explain to children what it meant to have to ride in the back of the bus.

We are not limited to biblical stories or modern parallels to those stories. Good use can also be made of works of fiction like Hans Christian Andersen's "There Is a Difference." That story is about a branch from an apple tree that is proud of its beautiful blossoms and looks down on a lowly dandelion, which it dismisses as "just a weed." "I suppose there have to be weeds," it says, "but I am very grateful that I was not born one of them." But a young countess who admires the apple blossoms also admires a single dandelion gone to seed, with its "perfect crown of white mist," and puts it on display in the castle alongside the apple branch. "Look how beautifully" God has made the dandelion, she says; it and the apple branch are different, "but they are both children of beauty."[6]

It is a wonderful story to go with the Parable of the Pharisee and the Tax Collector (although its point is subtly different) or to tell to children in the spring when both apple blossoms and dandelions can be brought as illustrations. And children, who appreciate beauty anywhere, will understand the story immediately. (I once watched while a young boy stood staring at a single dandelion for the longest time, lost in thought. If I were to tell the story, that boy would be on my mind as I prepared it.)

Our reading will reveal other useful stories similar to Andersen's, stories such as Raymond MacDonald Alden's *Why the Chimes Rang*; Shel Silverstein's *The Giving Tree*; Doris Stickney's *Water Bugs and Dragonflies*; and, for younger children, Margaret Wise Brown's *The Runaway Bunny*.[7] Some published stories would have to be abridged or simplified for use in a children's sermon, but that can be done while remaining faithful to the story's meaning.

Many kinds of stories can be used: biographical sketches, personal narratives, folktales. Fables and fairy tales are especially meaningful—fables, Hans Christian Andersen said, because the listener says without being told that "the fable is about me," and fairy tales because they "can give answers to the questions [we've] been thinking about."[8] Consider the story of "Beauty and the Beast," in which, as Frederick Buechner points out, "Beauty does not love the Beast because he is beautiful but makes him beautiful by loving him."[9] A parable of divine love in a form any child can understand.

Stories need not be literary; they can be found anywhere—in sports, for example. In the second quarter of the 1929 Rose Bowl game, the University of California's Roy Riegels picked up a fumble and *ran the wrong way* with the ball. He had to be tackled by a teammate or he would have scored for the other team. Although he was embarrassed and disappointed with himself, at halftime his coach simply told him to go out and play the second half. Roy did and played one of the best halves of his career. He was elected captain of the 1929 team, was given first team All-America honors, and eventually became a member of Cal's Athletic Hall of Fame.[10] That story of a second chance given after an embarrassing mistake fits perfectly with the Gospel and will be reassuring to the children who are sure they have made mistakes that no one can ever forgive or forget.

Even humorous stories have their place. Lyndon Johnson used to tell the story of a boy who said he had seen a lion in the back yard. His father went out and looked and saw that it was nothing more than the family's dog, Spot, and told the boy he ought to be ashamed of himself for telling stories like that. "Go upstairs, get down on your knees, and tell the Lord you're sorry for telling such a story," he said. When the boy came back downstairs, his father asked him if he had gotten down on his knees and told the Lord he was sorry. "Yes," the boy said. "And what did the Lord say?" "He said he thought it was a lion too."[11] Johnson used the story to speak about politicians who frighten the public by making lions out of things that are harmless. It speaks just as well to children's groundless fears.

Like Lyndon Johnson's story, some of the most useful stories are those within a child's experience. Harold Steindam tells a story about a boy playing the innkeeper in a Christmas pageant who forgot his part and, following his feelings rather than the script, he told Mary and Joseph: "There's no place in the inn, but you can have my room!"[12] Not only is the story close to a child's experience, but a child will readily understand that the boy's willingness to let the Holy Family in is more important than getting the pageant right.

Stories are available in abundance; how does one choose among them for use in children's sermons? Some of the criteria for choosing are the same as we would use with stories for adults: selecting stories with stimulating thoughts, vividness or beauty of expression, and believable characters; and, on the other hand, avoiding hackneyed stories, sentimental stories, and stories with assumptions about people and life that don't ring true. In some cases, however, stories well-suited for adults will not be useful with children: stories that rely on symbolism or irony, for example. O. Henry's "The Gift of the Magi" is a wonderful story, but its irony and reliance on adult experience make it an unlikely choice for children.

Still other stories, although suitable for children, seem to me poor choices for children's sermons, especially those that simply encourage moral behavior. "The Little Engine That Could" is a classic example of such a story. It teaches perseverance in an unforgettable way, but perseverance itself is not the most important thing we could be talking about with children. The most important thing is the Gospel, and the best stories are those that proclaim the Gospel or help to understand some aspect of it.

We can enrich children's lives by including stories from different countries and different cultures, and perhaps from unfamiliar parts of our own country—farms, inner cities, reservations—with their varied cultures. Those stories, even without our commentary, will help children identify with people they might not ordinarily meet and realize that they too are among God's people.

Some ministers write their own stories. Knowing the children they will be speaking to, they can write the stories so they are an exact fit for the ages and the needs of the children who will be present. Many of us could relate meaningful stories out of our own experience that would be just as effective as anything we might find in a book. Two of my experiences provided stories that were useful in speaking to children.

When I was a boy, I loved to sleep outside, to get together with my friends, take our sleeping bags and some hot dogs and head for the local woods. Once, when two of us had planned to sleep out, I asked my father if I could go, and he flatly said, "No!" I don't think he said why, but I may not have been listening. I went to bed that night very angry at my father for being so mean, so unfair and unfeeling. The next morning, I awoke to see snow. There must have been six or eight inches of snow on the ground—and I was sort of glad that we hadn't been sleeping outside; we might have frozen. My father had apparently heard the weather report and, against my wishes, had kept us safe. Children sometimes wonder why their prayers go unanswered. I can't tell them why, but I can tell them a story that suggests a reason.

I was once at a church office when a rather seedy-looking man with a paper bag came to the door and was cautiously let in. He had found a gerbil (he called it a mouse) in a box with the church's name on it, watched over it for two hours, and when no one came for it, brought it to the office, thinking it would be well taken care of there. (It was, even though it didn't belong to the church.) The next day, the man came back to see how "the mouse" was doing. Children today are not familiar with sheep and shepherds, but they could easily relate to the story of the lost gerbil and to the real gerbil I showed them on Sunday morning, and at the same time they learned something about the surprising compassion of a seedy-looking man with a paper bag.

Perhaps you have stories to tell, too: incidents from your life that shed light on biblical truths; or events that inspired you or brought you closer to God—the personal, sacred stories of your life.

Some ministers, believing that children learn best "experientially," using all their senses, have them act stories out. One Sunday, the children may crawl, walk, run, and hobble down the aisle to show how people of different ages move toward the cross on their faith journey. Another Sunday, the minister may lead the children out of the church by one door and back in by another, while telling them how Moses led the people through the wilderness.[13] To learn how the disciples followed Jesus, the children may play Follow the Leader; they can "go in and out of rooms, weave around, run, hop, skip, turn in circles."[14] On Easter, children might race in pairs of two from the back to the front of the sanctuary to imitate Peter and John running to the tomb on the first Easter morning.[15]

I am less venturesome than these ministers. I think almost as much can be achieved by having the children use their imaginations while they remain in place—and with less disruption to the service. They can also learn "experientially" by handling objects and joining in conversations where they are. But if a minister wants to try a more "experiential" sermon and the congregation is willing, a few Sundays' trials should demonstrate how useful the method is.

Storytelling is an art that speaks with great power. In Sir Philip Sidney's words, a well-told story "holdeth children from play, and old men from the chimney corner."[16] Part of the power comes from the story itself and part from the storyteller, whose voice, gestures, emotions, and sincerity make the story come alive. And such a story, once heard, can find a lasting place in a listener's mind and soul. What follows are some suggestions about the art of storytelling that I have found useful.

It will help the children to know whether the stories we tell are true stories, things that really happened, or works of imagination. Children appreciate both kinds but may not know which are true and which are imaginary unless they are told. Of course, there is truth in works of imagination, or we would not be telling them, but that is a concept that would be difficult to communicate to most children.

Children have a limited sense of chronology. Telling them that something happened during the Reformation or in colonial days will mean little to them. But, without being too precise, it will help them to know whether the events in a story are old or new. Beginning the story with something like "a long time before your grandmother's grandmother was born"[17] or "just last week" will usually be sufficient.

Adults concern themselves with large themes in stories. Children are more interested in details, and a good storyteller knows that the story will become real for the children in its details. One of Hans Christian Andersen's biographers says that when Andersen told a story, he added the details that gave it life. "He didn't say, 'The children got into the carriage and then drove away.' No, he said, 'They got into the carriage—"good-bye, Dad! good-bye, Mum!"—the whip cracked smack! smack! and away they went, come on! gee-up!'" Instead of saying that a merchant was very rich, he said, "he was so rich that he could pave the whole street, and most of a little alley as well, with silver money."[18]

Make use of the children's imaginations. They love to pretend. "Let's pretend today. Let's pretend that we lived back when Jesus did, and that our parents let us get up close to Jesus and talk to him. And maybe show him our bikes and our new sneakers that light up when we walk. Jesus is glad to see us, and is very nice to us. Then while Jesus is talking to us, here come these big sourpuss men who chase us away. . . ." But then, don't be surprised if the children sometimes confuse their pretending with reality. A kindergartner, excited about the approach of Christmas, once told me he could feel Santa's reindeer licking his shoes under his chair!

We may not have much enthusiasm for the familiar stories we are expected to tell. The Christmas story, for example, has been told over and over again; what more can be said about it? But children are not bored with the Christmas story; it is still new to them. Engage some children in a conversation about Jesus' birth. They may get the shepherds and the wise men confused and may not know the difference between a manger and a stable, but note the awe in their voices as they tell the story and their tenderness as they pretend to lay the baby in the hay. It could renew your enthusiasm for telling what is admittedly an "old, old story."

The conventional wisdom is that we should not add a moral at the end of a story; we should leave it to the children to decide what the story means. And that is wise. We can trust children to understand our stories. And what is more, they will see their own hopes and fears reflected in the stories and begin to see possibilities for realizing their hopes and overcoming their fears.

Still, even though children can understand stories, they may not understand why the stories were told. They will understand the story about the Rose Bowl game without help but may not make the connection between the coach who gave Roy Riegels a second chance and the God who gives us second chances. A simple framework for the story may be useful, "two or three well-honed sentences to help the children make connections" as Ronald Mierzwa puts it.[19] "Who would have thought that Roy's coach would give him another chance to play—after a mistake like that? But here's something just as amazing: we have a God who always gives us another chance. God knows all about our mistakes but says, 'Let's forget about them. Go out and try again.'"

With or without such a framework, different children will get different things from our stories, perhaps things we did not intend. Bertrand Russell's beloved grandmother once read the Parable of the Prodigal Son at family prayers, and he said to her afterwards: "I know why you read that—because I broke my jug."[20] That may not be why his grandmother read the parable, but that is how a remorseful boy heard it.

Another boy also found unexpected meaning in a story. A hospital chaplain in Maine visited a young boy a few days before Christmas. Because the boy seemed unwilling to talk, the chaplain simply told him Luke's story of Jesus' birth. Surprisingly, the joyful story brought tears to the boy's eyes. The chaplain asked why he was crying, and he said: "It must have been awful lonely for the baby there in the manger." "It's awful lonely for you here, too, isn't it?" said the chaplain, and that began a conversation.[21]

Different responses to our stories are what we should expect. With children as with adults, different people get different things from any of our sermons. Out of a mixture of our words, the thoughts and experiences of the listeners, and the movement of God's Spirit, many messages may be heard—which is, to me, not only natural but a demonstration of the power and the mystery of preaching.

One of the most interesting comments about storytelling I know came from an old monk in Ethiopia. Well-versed in folk tales from childhood and accustomed to passing them on to children, he had ideas about the stories that apply to our storytelling on Sunday mornings:

> The tale must teach something important or I, an old man, would not bother to squat among noisy children to tell them stories. And then the tale must entertain, or children would not bother to squat down to listen to a dull, old man.[22]

~ 13 ~
Conversations

Children's sermons need not be monologues. They can include conversations with the children, opportunities to explore a subject with them in a Socratic manner rather than simply telling them what we have come to believe. Conversations have the advantage of allowing the children to participate by expressing their thoughts, while also allowing adults to learn what they are hearing and thinking. Conversations have the disadvantage of introducing the possibility of surprises—digressions and irrelevancies—and this means that one needs to prepare for them carefully.

Conversations are usually initiated by questions. The easiest and safest approach is to use questions in such a way that they give the sense of conversation without really encouraging the children to speak. Rhetorical questions do that: "We all forget to thank God sometimes, don't we?" "I'm sure you noticed how pretty it was this morning with the sun shining on the snow. Could anything be prettier than that?" A more meaningful question is one that is intended to encourage the children to think, even if not to express their thoughts. "Now you don't have to answer this. I just want you to think about it. What is the one thing you are most thankful for? Is it TV or your dog or your cat or your friends or your parents, or what? Think about that for a minute."

Factual questions are common because they too are safe and easy.

They require answers but answers that are brief and specific. "Who knows what special day we are celebrating today?" "What do you call the person who looks after sheep?" (Questions about children's interests or experiences, however, may not be as safe. Asking, "What are you going to wear for Halloween?" or "What did you get for Christmas?" may result in a barrage of answers that will be difficult to stop.)

Leading questions are safe but do little to create real conversation. "Don't you think church is the best place to be on Sunday morning?" expects only one answer, and children will dutifully provide it.

Open-ended questions, on the other hand, encourage real participation. "What kind of things can we pray about?" "What do you think we could do to welcome a new classmate?" "How do you think God feels when people call each other names?" Those questions are more risky; children may respond to them with inappropriate or irrelevant answers. But they are also more valuable because they encourage children to think and allow them to contribute their thoughts to the discussion. Note, however, that if the question is too broad children may not know how to answer it. "Why do we come to church?" may puzzle them, but if a narrower question is asked—"What are some of the things you like to do when you come to church?"—they are sure to have some ideas.

One interesting way to ask questions is to feign ignorance about something and to ask the children's help. "I saw all these lilies when I came into the church today and I don't know why they're here. Do you know how they got here or why they're here?" The children know that you know, but they enjoy the game and will eagerly tell you all they know about lilies and Easter Sunday.

Or playful questions can be asked. "Somebody said that Thursday was going to be Thanksgiving. Is that right? Is that the day that the man in a red suit comes? Is it the day you go trick-or-treating? What do you do on Thanksgiving?"

A more serious way to ask questions is to ask them in a wondering manner, as though something is missing and needs to be provided. "I know God answers prayers, but if you ask God for a bike so you can ride over to your grandma's house to help her with her yard work, would God really give you a bike? Is that something you can pray for?" Most children hearing questions asked like that are aware that something serious is being considered; one person said that after asking such a question "a deep thoughtfulness had rested upon the children."[1] And they will usually respond seriously, often with surprising and wonderful comments that help the sermon along.

A ministerial couple, Kathleen and Greg Bostrom, well aware of the unhelpful answers children sometimes give to questions, were apprehensive when their own son was old enough to participate in the children's sermon. But when his father asked where God was (was God in the church? in the sky?) their five-year-old son responded, to his parents' relief and amazement: "I have always believed that the whole world was in God's heart."[2]

When children respond with that kind of wisdom, their answers ought to be commended. "Yes, I hadn't thought of that, but that's a really good answer. I wish I *had* thought of it."

It may also be possible to build on the answers the children give.

"What are some of the things that make you think of God?"

"The trees."

"What about the trees?"

"They're so pretty. I could hug them."

"Yes, they are pretty. Could you make a pretty tree like the one with all the red leaves in front of the church? Could your parents? Could your teacher? A man once wrote a poem about trees. He said: 'Poems are made by fools like me, / But only God can make . . .' Yes, a tree."

Taking a child's comments seriously and enlarging on them will be deeply satisfying to the child and will encourage others to share their thoughts.

A child's comment may seem inappropriate or misinformed, but if we dismiss it too quickly, we may miss the reason for it in the child's mind. One Thanksgiving, Susan Johnson asked the children what they were thankful for. A little girl responded, "I am thankful for my baby sister." Johnson knew that the girl's mother was a single mother and that there was no baby in the family. When she asked, skeptically, "What baby sister?" the girl responded, "The one my dad and his new wife had."[3]

If answers are clearly wrong and need to be dealt with, it should be done gently: "No, I don't think Allah is a different God. Lots of people think that though, and I know some adults who would say exactly what you did. But 'Allah' is just the way you say 'God' in another language, in the Arabic language. 'Allah' and 'God' are just different ways of saying the same thing."

Sonja Stewart and Jerome Berryman suggest a different, more profound kind of questioning in worship, which they call "a time for wondering." It is time after a story that is used for "dialogue with the story, with one another, and with [the children's] experiences in the story," a time of openness to God's Spirit. The storyteller encourages reflection by asking "wondering" questions: "I wonder what it was like for Jesus to be alone in the desert for so long?" "I wonder how the sheep feel about the Good Shepherd?" The questions neither demand answers nor prohibit them. They are open to the children and their experiences of God in that moment. Conversation might build on a child's answer, or the answer might be left without comment as something to encourage even further wonderment.[4]

Gerard Pottebaum offers another useful way to ask questions. He doesn't ask, "What did Jesus say to the disciples at supper the night before he died?" which allows the children to answer while maintaining a distance from the story. Instead, he asks them to imagine they are at the table with Jesus and then asks, "How do you feel when you hear Jesus say, 'This is my body, which I am giving for you?'" That question invites the children into the story, makes them participants in it, and helps them discover relationships between the story and their own experiences.[5]

Harold Steindam takes a still different approach. He begins one of his published sermons by saying, "I have something to discuss with you this morning, and I want you to help me think about it." Then, with carefully prepared questions, he helps the children think through an ethical problem, acknowledging their "good ideas" at every point.[6] He could have simply presented the ideas himself, but his questions stimulate the children to think for themselves.

In whatever way conversations are conducted, the children deserve to have their contributions taken seriously. Most children will offer us their best—sometimes becoming our teachers—but even when their ideas seem shallow to us, we ought to respect them. We also ought to respect the children who eagerly ask to be heard and then, when called on, look at us blankly, unable to find the words to express what they are thinking. "It's hard to find the right words, isn't it? But I can see that you're thinking about it, and maybe you can tell me later what you're thinking." When children give faltering answers and we can guess what is meant, we may be able to assist them by rephrasing their comments so they can still feel they have made worthwhile contributions.

Children sometimes respond without using words, and their nonverbal responses also deserve our recognition. A minister once asked the children what "love" was. No one answered in words, but one little girl sat hugging her doll tightly. The minister didn't acknowledge her "answer," but he could easily have done so. "'Love' is hard to explain, isn't it? But Kayla knows what love is. Look how she hugs her doll, and how her doll hugs her. When you see hugs like that, that's love."[7]

Children may, of course, respond to our questions with questions of their own, and their questions also demand our respect. Children deserve honest answers to their questions. Not complete answers—they are not ready for theological discourses—but answers that are as true as we can provide and that will not need to be revised when the children are older.

Of course, we do not have all the answers, nor do we need to. Anna Jameson, writing in 1854, remembered hearing as a child "a very celebrated man profess his ignorance on some particular subject." An adult's admission of ignorance was so unusual to her, so surprising, that she "felt awe-struck—it gave me a perception of the infinite,—as when looking up at the starry sky." She came to believe that we should not try to give children all the answers but should "allow the unknown, the uncertain, the indefinite, to be suggested to their minds." That, she thought, would allow for the growth of a more "truly religious feeling" than "what we unadvisedly cram into a child's mind in the same form it has taken in our own."[8] Those thoughts may be unsettling to a preacher's mind but may also be worth considering.

Every Sunday some children will be present who neither answer nor ask questions, and some of those children may never participate. But they may still be listening and thinking. Our conversations with other children may provoke an internal dialogue in some quiet child with unforeseen results. Don't be surprised if that child questions you months later about things you had almost forgotten.

Sometimes, especially when only a few children are present, no one is willing to participate. Questions simply go unanswered. In that case, it may be best to use a different approach with the children, telling stories for example. Then, gradually, questions about the stories might be introduced, and as trust is built, some venturesome child may surprise us with answers to our questions.

Children's sermons that include conversations require ministers who can think on their feet in order to respond appropriately to what the children say. This is a skill that can be learned and that rewards our efforts to learn—but expect to make some mistakes along the way if you attempt it.

Puppets are sometimes used in a kind of conversation—characters as colorful as Chippy the Chimp, Samantha Skunk, and Harvey, a plush, pink hippopotamus.[9] The minister speaks with the puppet instead of speaking with the children. The children will delight in overhearing the conversation, and a thoughtful leader can introduce subjects and ideas into the conversation that the children might not think of or that might be awkward or embarrassing for them to introduce.

The children can, of course, also be engaged in conversation by the puppet, and they may feel free to say things to the puppet that they would not to an adult. There is a danger, however, that a conversation with a chimp, a skunk, or a hippopotamus may not be taken seriously by the children. A simple puppet made by tying a knot in a scarf will allow the children to imagine it in any way they like and may result in a more serious conversation.[10]

Still, whatever form the puppet takes, conversations between it and the children, as those between it and the leader, may serve a good purpose.

~ 14 ~
Interruptions

We are seldom interrupted when we preach to adults; adults are too polite for that. But children have not yet learned all the social graces, and interruptions are not only possible, they should be expected and prepared for.

If younger children are present, they may stand frozen in the aisle, not knowing what to do, or they may become frightened looking out at the congregation or be unhappy where they are seated. It may be enough to sit beside or hold such children, or it may be a kind thing to walk them back to their parents.

Younger children may also become physically disruptive, crying, dancing, crawling, climbing, and making it impossible to proceed. Their parents will be greatly embarrassed but may not know how or when to intervene. It is wise to have someone—perhaps a young person seated nearby—who is willing to assume the task of calming or removing a child when that seems necessary. It may also be useful to let parents know that they are welcome to come forward with their children or to sit nearby if they are unsure how their children will behave.

Older children may be disruptive in what they say. They may embarrass us by innocently saying what adults would only think: "You told us that before!" "You said 'Noah and the whale.' It was Jonah and the whale." The children may not be used to adults admitting their mistakes, but we ought to show them that that is possible.

A child of any age may begin to talk about something entirely unrelated to what is being discussed: panda bears, a new bicycle, a trip to Grandma's. Listen long enough to make sure that the comment is irrelevant—some of us take the long way around to say what we want to say—and if it is, try to deal with it tactfully. "That's a good point, but we're not talking about panda bears today. Remind me about that when we are talking about them." "Why don't you tell me about your new bike after church? I'd like to hear about it." "You'll have a good time at your Grandma's. I know she's a good cook."

What a child has to say, even if irrelevant, may sometimes be profound, perhaps a thought triggered in some curious way by something we said on an entirely different subject. "My mom says if you can't say something nice, don't say it." Take time to acknowledge the thought before moving on. "Your mother is very wise. You are blessed to have a mother like that."

Some children just can't wait to say something and sit on the edge of their seats, waving their hands furiously. We know they want to say something, but we don't know whether it is relevant or not. A useful strategy is to ignore the hands until after the point of the sermon has been made and then to call on them. If the comments prove to be irrelevant, they have not spoiled the message. Sometimes, of course, they are quite relevant and may reinforce what we were trying to say.

Sometimes, a child's comment will elicit a roar of laughter from the congregation. If, as is usually the case, the comment was made innocently, we ought to do what we can to save the child from embarrassment. "You're probably wondering why everyone laughed when you said your dad locked his keys in the car. It's because we've all done that. We're really laughing at ourselves for being so forgetful."

I think congregations can be coached on how to respond in situations like that. Funny things happen when children are present, but adults can be encouraged to chuckle to themselves rather than to laugh out loud and run the risk of embarrassing a child. Most adults have simply not thought about their reactions to the children and will respond well to some coaching. And when adults have learned to refrain from laughing at children's comments, their silence will also discourage the occasional child who is tempted to use the children's sermon to play the audience for laughs.

Some clergy have also not thought the matter through. One author suggests, for a sermon on the atonement, to have the children talk about times they and their brothers and sisters have been punished. "It can become a rather humorous conversation," he says, "especially as the parents listen and react."[1] Humorous, but embarrassing too, for both parents and children, and a kind of humor we should not encourage.

Sometime preachers are themselves disruptive. A child says excitedly that "my mommy has a baby in her tummy," and the preacher can't resist turning to the congregation and saying: "Kids say the darndest things!" There is seldom any good reason for making asides to the congregation during a children's sermon. Our attention ought to be focused on the children. But in any case, such asides should never be at a child's expense. If the child's comment was made innocently and honestly, it should be answered in the same way. "And some day soon you're going to be a big sister, aren't you? That's wonderful. I was a big sister, and it was just about the nicest thing that ever happened to me. I still love my baby sister, although she doesn't like me to call her 'my baby sister' any more."

No matter how thorough our preparation for the children's sermon, it may be some interruption that both the children and the adults will remember. If that happens, accept it with good grace—and as God's grace. God works through interruptions, too.

Epilogue
Sowers

~

MOST CHURCHGOERS LOVE CHILDREN'S sermons: the children running down the aisle at the minister's invitation certainly seem to; the adults craning their necks to get a better view of the children show that they do; and many of us who speak to children during worship find joy in doing so. But apart from the pleasure of the moment, do children's sermons have any lasting effect? Do they change the way the children think or feel?

Several studies have attempted to measure what children remember from children's sermons. In one study, thirty children were interviewed after church services, and only five of them—mostly younger children—did not remember what the children's sermon was about.[1] Another study, made in the 1930s, administered multiple-choice tests to children in the fifth, sixth, and seventh grades to see what they remembered. When children's sermons were read to them, the fifth graders remembered 54% of what they heard, the sixth graders 63%, and the seventh graders 70%. The author of that study declared the sermons a success if they were understood and remembered and a failure if they were not.[2]

The results of any sermon, however, are not so easily measured. A sermon may be remembered but without its message being understood. Or it may be remembered and understood without being taken seriously. A sermon may be remembered or understood only in part, but that part may have a life-changing effect. Even a *mis*understood sermon may affect a life. Testing children may be useful in finding out whether our language and methods are successfully conveying our message, but there are no tests for plumbing the depths of the heart to see what our sermons may have meant there.

Most of us will never know what effect we have had on the children. We will have to console ourselves with the thought that we are like the farmer in the parable, sowing seed in the hope that some of it will grow and bear fruit. Nevertheless, the responses of three very different children to words they heard in their childhood encourage me to think that what we say to children may have more profound effects than we could ever imagine.

Fanny Maltby was ten years old when a visiting minister spoke to her "Sabbath School" in Northampton, Massachusetts. The year was 1867, and the minister was Edward Parmelee Smith, an official of the American Missionary Association, which was then in the midst of a massive effort to provide schools and teachers for the newly freed slaves in the South.

Smith had been a parish minister in Pepperell, Massachusetts, before the Civil War and was accustomed to speaking to the children in Pepperell's Evangelical Congregational Church. He had a gift for speaking to children, and his children's sermons won him many friends. The children crowded around him whenever he walked down the street, some of them holding his hands and others holding onto his coattails.[3]

Smith spoke to the children in Northampton about the freed slaves' desire for education. Not only children but adults as well were eager to learn and were contributing all they could to the schools, but they needed help from their friends in the North. Teachers brave enough to teach among hostile southern whites were needed but so was money for buildings and books.

Fanny sat in the gallery with the other children in the "infant class" when Smith spoke. That evening she returned to hear him speak again and listened "with deep interest." But the very next day, she contracted "malignant scarlet fever," and the following day she was dead. A few days later, her pastor, S. E. Bridgman, wrote to Smith to tell him about Fanny's death. In a day when even children were not shielded from death, Fanny knew she was dying and said that she wanted to "will" the money she had in the savings bank, $16.22, "to educate the colored children."[4]

Bridgman was amazed at what Fanny had done. He told Smith that her family had lived in the South a great deal and that most of her mother's relatives were "of Southern tendencies & sympathies." The work of the American Missionary Association among the freed slaves was "the last object her mother especially would give to." But a minister with a gift for speaking to children had touched a young girl's heart.[5]

Ruby Bridges was six years old in 1960 when a federal judge ordered the integration of William Frantz Elementary School in New Orleans. Ruby was the first black child to attend the school. Escorted by four armed United States marshals, she passed a crowd that shouted and threatened her. For more than a year, she was the only child in her class, all the white families having withdrawn their children in protest.

Every day Ruby and the marshals had to walk to school through a taunting crowd. Yet Ruby simply smiled at them. Every day, coming and going, she stopped a few blocks from the school to pray for her tormentors:

> Please God, try to forgive those people.
> Because even if they say those bad things,
> They don't know what they're doing.
> So You could forgive them,
> Just like You did those folks a long time ago
> When they said terrible things about You.[6]

When an anxious psychiatrist, Robert Coles, asked her how she could do that, Ruby replied: "I go to church every Sunday, and we're told to pray for everyone, even the bad people, and so I do." When Coles prodded, she added: "They keep coming and saying the bad words, but my momma says they'll get tired after a while and then they'll stop coming. They'll stay home. The minister came to our house and he said the same thing, and not to worry, and I don't. The minister said God is watching and He won't forget, because He never does. The minister says if I forgive the people, and smile at them and pray for them, God will keep a good eye on everything and He'll be our protection."

Her minister told her that God chooses people to do his will, and she was willing to be "His Ruby" if that was what God wanted. For more than a year, Ruby walked to school with the marshals, and smiled, and prayed for those who shouted and spat at her. And in the end, some of the whites relented, and the school was finally integrated.[7]

The third child learned from a Catholic missal rather than a sermon, but his testimony shows in a different way how much a life can be affected by words first heard as a child.

Henry B. Gonzalez, the former U.S. congressman from Texas, was awarded the John F. Kennedy Profile in Courage Award in 1994 for his investigations of the savings and loan scandal and the sale of U.S. arms to Iraq. In his acceptance speech, he talked about his childhood as the son of immigrants from Mexico, and about the fear he had to contend with as a boy. "Fear seemed pervasive, hanging as a heavy fog all around my childhood world: the fear of abject poverty, of dread diseases like tuberculosis, and the fear linked to a hostile, alien neighborhood, speaking with a harsh and unfriendly sounding, incomprehensible language. There was the terror of being dragged to that first day of school—to its forbidding looking strange adults and unknown classmates; not knowing English, I was compelled to spend a whole year in 'low first' grade."[8]

Then one day, in his aunt's missal, he read these words by Santa Teresa de Jesús, which seemed to him "a heavenly message":

> Let nothing vex you
> Fear not.
> All things soon pass;
> Patience conquers all.
> He who has God with him wants for nothing,
> Our Lord God suffices.[9]

"From then on," Gonzalez said, "fear did not overwhelm me." He was able to face life with courage and, later, to speak out against injustice in a long career in public service—to be, as he put it, "a thorn in the side of unprincipled privilege." And, one might add, to make an unprecedented contribution to American society. The courage he showed throughout his life, he said, was due to words he read in a missal as a boy.

Seeds often fall on rocky ground and produce nothing. But sometimes they fall into good soil and produce amazing results. Those who sow, whether seeds or words, do so in the faith that somewhere, somehow, God will produce a harvest.

A Prayer on Preparing to Speak to Children

~

God, be with me as I prepare to speak your Word to these children. Reassure me about the ability of children to understand and their capacity to believe, and make my faith equal to theirs. Then grant me the right words at the right time to satisfy the minds and gladden the hearts of these your children.

Amen.

Fry Graph for Estimating Readability—Extended

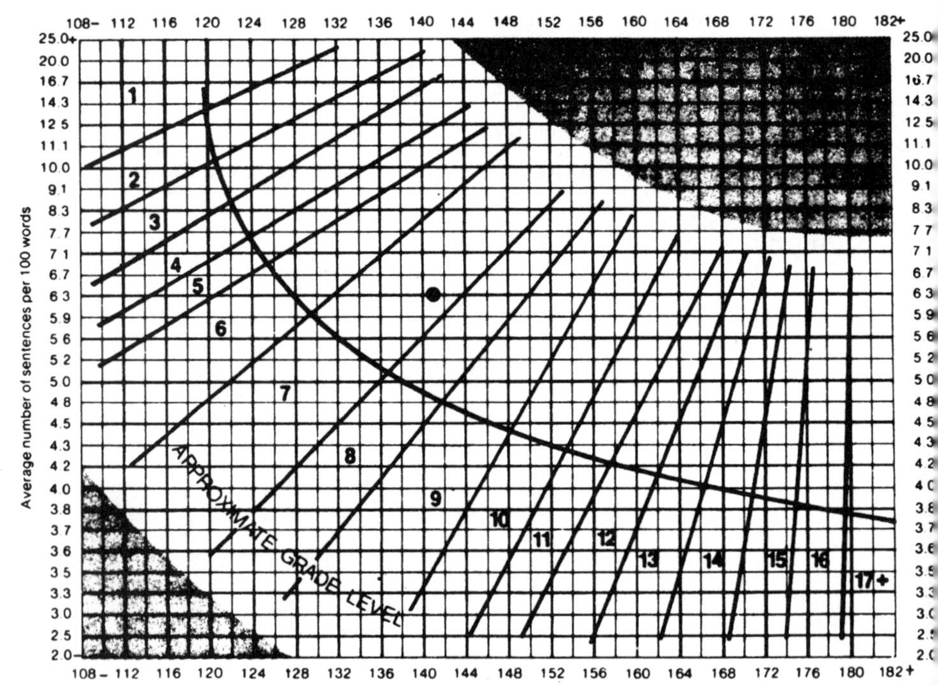

Appendix A[1]

~

DIRECTIONS:
Randomly select 3 one hundred word passages from a book or an article. Plot average number of syllables and average number of sentences per 100 words on graph to determine the grade level of the material. Choose more passages per book if great variability is oberved and conclude that the book has uneven readability. Few books will fall in gray area but when they do grade level scores are invalid.

Count proper nouns, numerals and initializations as words. Count a syllable for each symbol. For example, "1945" is 1 word and 4 syllables and "IRA" is 1 word and 3 syllables.

EXAMPLE:	SYLLABLES	SENTENCES
1st Hundred Words	124	6.6
2nd Hundred Words	141	5.5
3rd Hundred Words	158	6.8
Average	141	6.3

READABILITY 7TH GRADE (see dot plotted on graph)

Appendix B
"The Object Lesson"
BY JAMES WHITCOMB RILEY[1]

~

BARELY A YEAR AGO I ATTENDED THE FRIDAY afternoon exercises of a country school. My mission there, as I remember, was to refresh my mind with such material as might be gathered, for a "valedictory," which, I regret to say, was to be handed down to posterity under another signature than my own.

There was present, among a host of visitors, a pale young man of perhaps thirty years, with a tall head and bulging brow and a highly-intellectual pair of eyes and spectacles. He wore his hair without roach or "part" and the smile he beamed about him was "a joy forever." He was an educator—from the East, I think I heard it rumored—anyway he was introduced to the school at last, and he bowed, and smiled, and beamed upon us all, and entertained us after the most delightfully edifying manner imaginable. And although I may fail to reproduce the exact substance of his remarks upon that highly important occasion, I think I can at least present his theme in all its coherency of detail. Addressing more particularly the primary department of the school, he said:—

"As the little exercise I am about to introduce is of recent origin, and the bright, intelligent faces of the pupils before me seem rife with eager and expectant interest, it will be well for me, perhaps, to offer by way of preparatory preface a few terse words of explanation.

"The Object-Lesson is designed to fill a long-felt want, and is destined, as I think, to revolutionize, in a great degree, the educational systems of our land.—In my belief, the Object-Lesson will supply want which I may safely say has heretofore left the most egregious and palpable traces of mental confusion and intellectual inadequacies stamped, as it were, upon the gleaming reasons of the most learned—the highest cultured, and the most eminently gifted and promising of our professors and scientists both at home and abroad.

"Now this deficiency—if it may be so termed—plainly has a beginning; and probing deeply with the bright, clean scalpel of experience we discover that—"As the twig is bent, the tree's inclined." To remedy, then, a deeply-seated error which for so long has rankled at the very root of educational progress throughout the land, many plausible, and we must admit, many helpful theories have been introduced to allay the painful errors resulting from the discrepancy of which we speak: but until now, nothing that seemed wholly to eradicate the defect has been discovered, and that, too, strange as it may seem, is, at last, found emanating, like the mighty river, from the simplest source, but broadening and gathering in force and power as it flows along, until, at last, its grand and mighty current sweeps on in majesty to the vast illimitable ocean of—of—of—Success! Ahem!

"And, now, little boys and girls, that we have had by implication, a clear and comprehensive explanation of the Object-Lesson and its mission, I trust you will give me your undivided attention while I endeavor—in my humble way—to direct your newly acquired knowledge through the proper channel. For instance:—

"This little object I hold in my hand—who will designate it by its proper name? Come, now, let us see who will be the first to answer. 'A peanut,' says the little boy here at my right. Very good—very good! I hold, then, in my hand, a peanut. And now who will tell me, what is the peanut? A very simple question—who will answer? 'Something good to eat,' says the little girl. Yes, 'something good to eat,' but would it not be better to say simply that the peanut is an edible? I think so, yes. The peanut, then, is—an edible—now, all together, an edible!

"To what kingdom does the peanut belong? The animal, vegetable or mineral kingdom? A very easy question. Come, let us have prompt answers. 'The animal kingdom,' does the little boy say? Oh, no! The peanut does not belong to the animal kingdom! Surely the little boy must be thinking of a larger object than the peanut—the elephant, perhaps. To what kingdom, then, does the peanut belong? The v-v-veg—'The vegetable kingdom,' says the bright-faced little girl on the back seat. Ah! that is better. We find then that the peanut belongs to the—what kingdom? The 'vegetable kingdom.' Very good, very good!

"And now who will tell us of what the peanut is composed. Let us have quick responses now. Time is fleeting! Of what is the peanut composed? 'The hull and the goody,' some one answers. Yes, 'the hull and the goody' in vulgar parlance, but how much better it would be to say simply, the shell and the kernel. Would not that sound better? Yes, I thought you would agree with me there!

"And now who will tell me the color of the peanut? And be careful now! for I shouldn't like to hear you make the very stupid blunder I once heard a little boy make in reply to the same question. Would you like to hear what color the stupid little boy said the peanut was? You would, eh? Well, now, how many of you would like to hear what color the stupid little boy said the peanut was? Come now, let's have an expression. All who would like to hear what color the stupid little boy said the peanut was, may hold up their right hands. Very good, very good—there, that will do.

"Well, it was during a professional visit I was once called upon to make to a neighboring city, where I was invited to address the children of a free school—Hands down, now, little boy—founded for the exclusive benefit of the little newsboys and bootblacks, who, it seems, had not the means to defray the expenses of the commonest educational accessories, and during an object lesson identical with the one before us now—for it is a favorite one of mine—I propounded the question, what is the color of the peanut? Many answers were given in response, but none as sufficiently succinct and apropos as I deemed the facts demanded; and so at last I personally addressed a ragged, but, as I then thought, a bright-eyed little fellow, when judge of my surprise, in reply to my question, what is the color of a peanut, the little fellow, without the slightest gleam of intelligence lighting up his face, answered, that 'if not scorched by roasting, the peanut was a blond.' Why, I was almost tempted to join in the general merriment his inapposite reply elicited. But I occupy your attention with trivial things; and as I notice the time allotted me has slipped away, we will drop the peanut for the present. Trusting the few facts gleaned from a topic so homely and unpromising will sink deep in your minds, in time to bloom and blossom in the fields of future usefulness—I—I—I thank you."

Notes

~

Preface

1. Jay T. Stocking, *The Child in the Congregation* (Boston: The Pilgrim Press, 1929), p. 66.

Introduction: *Why Children's Sermons?*

1. Hans Christian Andersen, *The Complete Fairy Tales and Stories*, trans. Erik Christian Haugaard (New York: Anchor Books, 1974), pp. 414-15.

2. Carolyn C. Brown, *You Can Preach to the Kids Too! Designing Sermons for Adults and Children* (Nashville: Abingdon, 1997), pp. 19, 21, 28 et passim.

PART ONE: CHILDREN

Chapter One: *Children's Thoughts*

1. Ina Hughs, *A Prayer for Children* (New York: William Morrow and Co., 1995), p. xv.

2. Carl Renz and Mildred Paul Renz, *Big Problems on Little Shoulders* (New York: The Macmillan Co., 1934). William Golding's *Lord of the Flies* (New York: Riverhead Books, 1997) gives a darker view of children's lives, picturing not only "the end of innocence" but also "the darkness of man's heart" (p. 235) in a group of boys from six to twelve years old.

3. Robert Coles, *The Spiritual Life of Children* (Boston: Houghton Mifflin Co., 1990), p. 37. Gauguin's painting is discussed in David Sweetman, *Paul Gauguin: A Life* (New York: Simon & Schuster, 1995), pp. 454-59.

4. Robert Louis Stevenson, "Child's Play" in Roger Ricklefs, ed., *The Mind of Robert Louis*

Stevenson: Selected Essays, Letters, and Prayers (New York: Thomas Yoseloff, 1963), p. 38.

5. Henry Wadsworth Longfellow, "My Lost Youth" in *The Complete Poetical Works of Longfellow* (Boston: Houghton Mifflin Co., 1893), pp. 193-95.

6. Penelope Fitzgerald, *The Knox Brothers* (Washington, DC: Counterpoint, 2000), pp. 34-35.

7. Bertrand Russell, *The Autobiography of Bertrand Russell* (Boston: Little, Brown and Co., 1967), 1:14.

8. John Townsend Trowbridge, *My Own Story: With Recollections of Noted Persons* (Boston: Houghton Mifflin and Co., 1903), pp. 23-24.

9. Walter De la Mare, *Early One Morning in the Spring: Chapters on Children and on Childhood as It Is Revealed in Particular in Early Memories and in Early Writings* (1935; repr., New York: Octagon Books, 1977), pp. 199-200.

10. Gareth B. Matthews, *The Philosophy of Childhood* (Cambridge, MA: Harvard University Press, 1994), p. 1.

11. Gareth B. Matthews, *Philosophy and the Young Child* (Cambridge, MA: Harvard University Press, 1980), p. 36.

12. Phyllis Vos Wezeman, Anna L. Liechty, and Kenneth R. Wezeman, *Wipe the Tears: 30 Children's Sermons on Death* (Cleveland: The Pilgrim Press, 2004), p. 13.

13. 1 Cor. 3:2.

14. Russell, *Autobiography*, 1:19.

15. Paul Steinberg, *Speak You Also: A Survivor's Reckoning*, trans. Linda Coverdale with Bill Ford (New York: Metropolitan Books/Henry Holt & Co., 2000), pp. 34-36.

16. Anne Neufeld Rupp, *Growing Together: Understanding and Nurturing Your Child's Faith Journey* (Newton, KS: Faith and Life Press, 1996), p. 102.

17. Matt. 12:36.

18. Charles Dickens, *My Early Times*, comp. and ed. Peter Rowland (London: The Folio Society, 1988), p.78.

19. Kenneth Grahame, *The Golden Age* (New York: Dodd, Mead & Co., 1929), p. 110. Carole Shields writes at length about her confused thoughts as a child in *Unless* (New York: Fourth Estate, 2002), pp. 92-101.

CHAPTER TWO: *Children's Thoughts about Religion*

1. Edward Robinson, *The Original Vision: A Study of the Religious Experience of Childhood* (New York: Seabury Press, 1983), p. 97.

2. *Wie anders, Gretchen, war dir's,*

Als du noch voll Unschuld
Hier zum Altar trat'st,
Aus dem vergriffnen Büchelchen
Gebete lalltest,
Halb Kinderspiele,
Halb Gott im Herzen!

Johann Wolfgang von Goethe, *Faust*, Part I, "Dom," lines 3776-82.

3. Coles, *The Spiritual Life of Children*, pp. xvi, 168-69, 289-90. See also Coles's *The Moral Intelligence of Children* (New York: Random House, 1997) and *The Moral Life of Children* (Boston: Atlantic Monthly Press, 1986).

4. Coles, *The Spiritual Life of Children*, p. 329.

5. Kathryn Harrison, *Saint Thérèse of Lisieux: A Penguin Life* (New York: Lipper/Viking, 2003), p. 58.

6. Trowbridge, *My Own Story,* p. 31.

7. Albert Schweitzer, *Memoirs of Childhood and Youth*, trans. C. T. Campion (New York: The Macmillan Co., 1931), p. 40.

8. Ibid., pp. 23-24, 61.

9. Edward Hoffman, *Visions of Innocence: Spiritual and Inspirational Experiences of Childhood* (Boston: Shambhala, 1992); Robinson, *The Original Vision.*

10. Hoffman, *Visions of Innocence*, p. 46.

11. Robert J. Landy, *How We See God and Why It Matters: A Multicultural View Through Children's Drawings and Stories* (Springfield, IL: Charles C. Thomas, 2001), p. 172. Note too, Reynolds Price's account of a vision of "one giant wheel of all created things" given to him at the age of six or seven in his *Letter to a Godchild: Concerning Faith* (New York: Scribner, 2006), pp. 23-30.

12. Kathleen Norris, *Dakota: A Spiritual Geography* (Boston: Houghton Mifflin Co., 1993), p. 21. See also Norris's poem "The Sky Is Full of Blue and Full of the Mind of God" in her *Little Girls in Church* (Pittsburgh: University of Pittsburgh Press, 1995), p. 50.

13. Walt Whitman, *Complete Poetry and Collected Prose* (New York: Library of America, 1982), p. 412.

14. Calvin Trillin, *Family Man* (New York: Farrar, Straus and Giroux, 1998), p. 108.

15. Ana-Maria Rizzuto, *The Birth of the Living God: A Psychoanalytic Study* (Chicago: University of Chicago Press, 1979), p. 8. See also Eileen W. Lindner, "Children as Theologians" in Peter B. Pufall and Richard P. Unsworth, eds., *Rethinking Childhood* (New Brunswick, NJ: Rutgers University Press, 2004), pp. 54-68.

CHAPTER THREE: *Respect for Children*

1. *Maxima debetur puero reverentia.*

Juvenal, Satires 14, line 47.

2. James Whitcomb Riley, "The Raggedy Man on Children" in *The Complete Works of James Whitcomb Riley* (New York, Harper & Brothers, 1916), 8:2236.

3. Parker Rossman, "Children Who Listen," *The Christian Ministry* 16 (Jan. 1985): 16-17.

CHAPTER FOUR: *Deepening Our Understanding of Children*

1. O. Suthern Sims Jr., *Creating and Leading Children's Sermons: A Developmental Approach* (Macon, GA: Smyth & Helwys, 1999); Sara Covin Juengst, *Sharing Faith with Children: Rethinking the Children's Sermon* (Louisville, KY: Westminster John Knox Press, 1994).

2. Gareth B. Matthews, *Dialogues with Children* (Cambridge, MA: Harvard University Press, 1984). See especially pp. 116-19. See also Matthews's *Philosophy of Childhood*, pp. 16-18, 30-40. On pages 54-67 of the *Philosophy* book, Matthews also criticizes developmental psychologists' ideas about the stages of moral development.

3. School and the playground can also be visited through books such as Tracy Kidder, *Among Schoolchildren* (New York: Avon Books, 1989), and Iona Opie, *The People in the Playground* (New York: Oxford University Press, 1993).

4. Trowbridge, *My Own Story*, p. 444. Longfellow's playfulness with children is also seen in his poem "The Children's Hour." See *Poems and Other Writings* (New York: The Library of America, 2000), pp. 347-48.

5. Michael Burlingame, *The Inner World of Abraham Lincoln* (Urbana: University of Illinois Press, 1994), p. 58.

6. June Jordan, *Soldier: A Poet's Childhood* (New York: Basic Civitas Books, 2000), pp. 59, 61.

7. Maryse Condé, *Tales from the Heart: True Stories from My Childhood*, trans. Richard Philcox (New York: Soho Press, 2001), pp. 46-47.

8. Julia Collins, *My Father's War: A Memoir* (New York: Four Walls Eight Windows, 2002); Yolanda Young, *On Our Way to Beautiful: A Family Memoir* (New York: Villard, 2002); Dickens, *My Early Times*: Lucy Larcom, *A New England Girlhood: Outlined from Memory* (Boston: Houghton Mifflin and Co., 1889); Russell, *Autobiography*; Schweitzer, *Memoirs*; George Orwell, "Such, Such Were the Joys . . ." in *A Collection of Essays* (New York: Harcourt Brace & Co., 1981), pp. 1-47.

9. Herman Melville, *Redburn: His*

First Voyage (Garden City, NY: Doubleday Anchor Books, 1957), pp. 9–10.

10. Antoine De Saint-Exupéry, *The Little Prince*, trans. Richard Howard (New York: Harcourt, 2000), dedication.

11. Richard Bromfield, *Living with the Boogeyman: Helping Your Child Cope with Fear, Terrorism, and Living in a World of Uncertainty* (Roseville, CA: Prima Publishing, 2002).

12. Kurt Heinecke/Phil Vischer, "God Is Bigger Than the Boogeyman" (Franklin, TN: Big Idea, Inc. c. Bob and Larry Publishing (ASCAP), 1993).

PART TWO: MESSAGE

Chapter Five: *More Than a Lesson*

1. Albert Schweitzer, *The Quest of the Historical Jesus: A Critical Study of Its Progress from Reimarus to Wrede* (New York: The Macmillan Co., 1948), p. 401.

2. Christina Rossetti, "A Christmas Carol" in *The Complete Poems of Christina Rossetti*, ed. R. W. Crump (Baton Rouge: Louisiana State University Press, 1979–1990), 1:216–17.

3. Fred B. Craddock, *Craddock Stories*, ed. Mike Graves and Richard F. Ward (St. Louis, MO: Chalice Press, 2001), pp. 37–38.

4. Robert Coles, *Their Eyes Meeting the World: The Drawings and Paintings of Children*, ed. Margaret Sartor (Boston: Houghton Mifflin Co., 1992), pp. 90–91.

Chapter Six: *Sharing the Faith*

1. Herbert Anderson and Susan B. W. Johnson, *Regarding Children: A New Respect for Childhood and Families* (Louisville, KY: Westminster John Knox Press, 1994), p. 124.
2Rochelle Melander and Harold Eppley, *Dancing in the Aisle: Spiritual Lessons We've Learned from Children>* (Cleveland: United Church Press, 1999), pp. 121–23.

3. See D. Raye Jones, "A Child in Their Midst: Strengthening the Children's Sermon" (DMin dissertation, Columbia Theological Seminary, 1999), p. 69.

4. Glen E. Rainsley, *Small Wonders: Sermons for Children* (Cleveland: United Church Press, 1998), p. xvi.

5. Stan Stewart and Pauline Hubner, *Talking about Something Important* (Melbourne: The Joint Board of Christian Education of Australia and New Zealand, 1981), pp. 123–24.

6. Amy Hollingsworth, *The Simple Faith of Mister Rogers: Spiritual Insights from the World's Most Beloved Neighbor* (Nashville:

Integrity Publishers, 2005), p. 51.

CHAPTER SEVEN: *Preparing the Message*

1. Cynthia Pearl Maus, *Christ and the Fine Arts* (New York: Harper & Brothers, 1938), pp. 668–72.

2. Jacqueline Briggs Martin, *Snowflake Bentley* (Boston: Houghton Mifflin Co., 1998); Jericho Historical Society, http://snowflakebentley.com/index.html (accessed September 14, 2006).

3. Stewart and Hubner, *Talking about Something Important.*

4. Matt. 12:20.

5. Halford E. Luccock, *Like a Mighty Army: Selected Letters of Simeon Stylites* (New York: Oxford University Press, 1954), p. 40.

6. Siegfried Rabus, *Die Kinderpredigt: Problem und Bestand einer kindgemässen Sprache der Kirche* (Hamburg: Furche-Verlag, 1967), pp. 48–49; Stefan Welz, *Die Kinderpredigt: Zur Predigtlehre und Praxis eines Verkündigungsmodells* (Hooksiel: Jade Verlag, 2001), pp. 12–16.

7. Samuel Phillips, *Children Well Imployed, and, Jesus Much Delighted; . . . a Plain Discourse Lately Preach'd to the Children of the South-Parish in Andover . . .* (Boston: S. Kneeland and T. Green, for D. Henchman in Cornhill, 1739); H. Clay Trumbull, *The Sunday-School: Its Origin, Mission, Methods, and Auxiliaries* (Philadelphia: John D. Wattles & Co., 1896), pp. 321–27, 333–35.

8. John C. Hill, *The Children's Sermon. With a Selection of Five Minute Sermons to Children, for Pastors, Sunday-School Libraries and Home Reading* (Philadelphia: Presbyterian Board of Publication, 1882), pp. 11–12; Trumbull, *The Sunday-School*, pp. 327–33.

PART THREE: METHODS

CHAPTER EIGHT: *The Setting*

1. Larry S. Grounds, "To Such as These: How to Design and Present Children's Stories for Congregational Worship" (DMin dissertation project, San Francisco Theological Seminary, 2002), pp. 66, 78.

2. Charles R. Case, "An Investigation into the Functional Values of the Children's Sermon within the Framework of the Morning Worship Service" (DMin thesis project, Eastern Baptist Theological Seminary, 1981), p. 139.

3. Stewart and Hubner, *Talking about Something Important*, pp. 26–27. In a further step in a small congregation, on at least one occasion the adults and children were divided into groups of five for joint conversations on the topic of the talk to the children. See pp. 97–99.

4. Charles Roads, *Little Children in the Church of Christ* (Boston: D. Lothrop Co., 1893), p. 14.

5. Fred Craddock suggested this interpretation in his *Overhearing the Gospel* (Nashville: Abingdon, 1978), p. 109.

6. Bob Barber, "Handling Children's Object Lessons," *The Christian Ministry* 18 (Sept.-Oct. 1987), p. 24.

7. Stanley Nance Blevins, "The Children's Sermon as a Basis for Spiritual Dialogue between Parents and Children" (DMin professional project report, Southwestern Baptist Theological Seminary, 1982).

8. Hugh Smith III, "Creating Children's Stories That Work in Worship for Children and the Child Within" (DMin thesis project report, Princeton Theological Seminary, 1992). Another way of providing dialogue about the children's sermon is to have a classroom discussion of it among children who do not remain for the entire worship service.

9. Trumbull, *The Sunday-School*, p. 327.

10. Raimundo De Ovies, *The Church and the Children* (New York: Morehouse-Gorham Co., 1941), p. 171.

11. Philip Daniel Schroeder, "From Illustration to Animation: Modeling a Paradigm Shift in Worship and Homiletics through Children's Sermons" (DMin thesis, United Theological Seminary, 1995), p. 83.

12. Marion Gerard Gosselink, *52 Three Minute Talks to Children* (Boston: W. A. Wilde Co., 1961); Gerard Benjamin Fleet Hallock, *Three Hundred Five-Minute Sermons for Children* (Garden City, NY: Doubleday, Doran & Co., 1928).

13. *Quick Children's Sermons*, 4 vols. (Loveland, CO: Group Publishing, 1997-2003); Vicky Miller and Deborah Raney, *Children's Sermons to Go: 52 Take-Home Lessons about God* (Nashville: Abingdon, 1998); Paul E. Holdcraft, *101 Snappy Sermonettes for the Children's Church* (New York: Abingdon-Cokesbury Press, 1951).

CHAPTER NINE: *Language*

1. John W. Etter, *The Preacher and His Sermon: A Treatise on Homiletics* (Dayton, OH: United Brethren Publishing House, 1885), p. 256.

2. S. Lawrence Johnson, *The Cross-Eyed Bear and Other Children's Sermons* (Nashville: Abingdon, 1980), p. 23.

3. A useful overview is provided in Beverley L. Zakaluk and S. Jay Samuels, eds., *Readability: Its Past, Present, and Future*(Newark, DE:

International Reading Assoc., 1988).

4. William Shakespeare, Sonnet 18, lines 13–14.

5. Thomas H. Johnson, ed., *The Complete Poems of Emily Dickinson* (Boston: Little Brown and Co., 1960), pp. 534–35. A. E. Housman is another poet who created some memorable poems using mostly one-syllable words.

6. Vivian Gussin Paley, *Wally's Stories* (Cambridge, MA: Harvard University Press, 1981), p. 173.

7. Elizabeth P. Peabody, *Lectures in the Training Schools for Kindergartners* (Boston: D. C. Heath & Co., 1906), pp. 102–3.

8. Iona and Peter Opie, eds., *I Saw Esau: The Schoolchild's Pocket Book* (Cambridge, MA: Candlewick Press, 1992), p. 21.

9. From Robert Grant's text for the hymn "O Worship the King, All Glorious Above."

10. This is the title of a Brian Wren hymn (Carol Stream, IL: Hope Publishing Co., 1989, rev. 1994).

11. Clarence Day, *God and My Father* (New York: Alfred A. Knopf, 1935), pp. 27–28.

CHAPTER TEN: *Objects*

1. C. W. Bess, *Children's Object Sermons for the Seasons* (Grand Rapids, MI: Baker Book House, 1993); Dorothy Brenner Francis, *Promises and Turtle Shells: and 49 other Object Lessons for Children* (Nashville: Abingdon, 1984); Arnold Carl Westphal, *Junior Surprise Sermons with Hand-made Objects* (New York: Fleming H. Revell Co., 1943); Jessie P. Sullivan, *Object Lessons with Easy-to-Find Objects* (Grand Rapids, MI: Baker Books, 1981).

2. Bucky Dann, *Creating Children's Sermons: 51 Visual Lessons* (Philadelphia: Westminster Press, 1981), p. 21.

3. J. Russell Cross, "Preaching to Children" (ThM thesis, Louisville Presbyterian Seminary, 1938), p. 26.

4. Bess, *Object-centered Children's Sermons*, pp. 101–2.

5. Dann, *Creating Children's Sermons*, pp. 66–67.

6. Luther S. Cross, *Easy Object Stories* (Grand Rapids, MI: Baker Book House, 1984), pp. 86–88.

7. William Shakespeare, *A Midsummer Night's Dream*, V, i, lines 16–17.

8. Helen Clarke, ed., *Children's Prayers Around the World* (Richmond, VA: Christian Children's Fund, 1959), p. 37.

9. Kenneth L. Chafin, *The Reluctant Witness* (Nashville: Broadman Press, 1974), p. 109.

10. Francis T. Cancro, "To Live the

Word with Little Folks," in Frank J. McNulty, ed., *Preaching Better* (New York: Paulist Press, 1985), p. 100.

11. Andersen, *The Complete Fairy Tales and Stories*, pp. 259-60.

12. See Jerry Marshall Jordan, *Filling Up the Brown Bag (A Children's Sermon How-to Book)* (Cleveland: The Pilgrim Press 1987).

13. Elizabeth Barrett Browning, *Aurora Leigh*, ed. Margaret Reynolds (Athens: Ohio University Press, 1992), p. 487.

14. Helen Dukas and Banesh Hoffmann, eds., *Albert Einstein: The Human Side: New Glimpses from His Archives* (Princeton: Princeton University Press, 1979), pp. 19, 165. Einstein said to an eighty-year-old friend late in his own life that the two of them still stood "like curious children before the great Mystery into which we are born." Ibid., pp. 82, 150.

15. Whitman, *Complete Poetry*, pp. 803-5.

16. William Blake, *The Complete Poetry and Prose of William Blake*, rev. ed., David V. Erdman, editor (New York: Anchor Books, 1988), p. 490.

17. Alfred Tennyson, "Flower in the Crannied Wall" in *The Complete Poetical Works of Tennyson* (Boston: Houghton Mifflin Co., 1898), p. 274.

18. John Perry, *Unshakable Faith* (Sisters, OR: Multnomah Publishers, 1999), p. 286.

19. Rachel Carson, *The Sense of Wonder*, photog. William Neill (Berkeley, CA: The Nature Company, 1956, 1990). The pages are unnumbered. Barry Lopez describes a similar approach to children in "Children in the Woods" in his *Crossing Open Ground* (New York: Charles Scribner's Sons, 1988), pp. 147-51.

20. Millicent Todd Bingham, *Emily Dickinson's Home: Letters of Edward Dickinson and His Family* (New York: Harper & Brothers, 1955), p. 171.

21. Barbara Brown Taylor, *The Preaching Life* (Cambridge, MA: Cowley Publications, 1993), pp. 14-15.

22. Alpha and Omega Christian Bookstore, http://bankhead.net/alpha/education.html, (accessed September 12, 2006).

23. Henry Sloane Coffin, *The Public Worship of God: A Source Book* (Philadelphia: The Westminster Press, 1946), pp. 170-72.

24. Cynthia L. LaRusch, comp., *Sermons from the Mystery Box as Told by R. Douglas Reinard* (Nashville: Abingdon, 1991), pp. 9-10.

25. Stuart Hample and Eric

Marshall, comp., *Children's Letters to God: The New Collection* (New York: Workman Publishing, 1991). The pages are unnumbered.

26. The bananas are in Jordan, *Filling Up the Brown Bag*, pp. 65–67; the pickle and the soda can are in Guy Stewart, *Simple Science Sermons for Big and Little Kids* (Lima, OH: CSS Publishing Co. 1998), pp. 13–14, 27–28.

CHAPTER ELEVEN: *Analogies*

1. Jerry Marshall Jordan, *One More Brown Bag (Of Sermons for Children)* (New York: The Pilgrim Press, 1983), p. 110.

2. See Jordan, *Filling Up the Brown Bag*, pp. 64–65.

3. Brant D. Baker, *Let the Children Come: A New Approach to Children's Sermons* (Minneapolis: Augsburg, 1991), pp. 40–41. In his *Welcoming the Children: Experiential Children's Sermons* (Minneapolis: Augsburg, 1995), p. 8, Baker says that "we should not expect children ages two through ten to make analogical jumps—*this* is like *that*. . . ." But some of his experiential sermons, like this one, have an implicit analogy in them. I think children can understand some comparisons, but the comparisons must be made explicit.

4. Jerry Marshall Jordan, *Another Brown Bag (Filled with Sermons for Children)* (New York: The Pilgrim Press, 1980), pp. 109–10.

5. Rainsley, *Small Wonders*, pp. 46–47, 74–75.

6. Sims, *Creating and Leading Children's Sermons*, p. 30.

7. Harold Steindam, *As the Twig Is Bent: Sermons for Children* (New York: The Pilgrim Press, 1983), pp. 78–79.

CHAPTER TWELVE: *Stories*

1. Dianne E. Deming, *A Time with Our Children: Stories for Use in Worship, Year B* (Cleveland: United Church Press, 1993), pp. 92–93.

2. Søren Kierkegaard, *Fear and Trembling*, trans. Alastair Hannay (New York: Penguin Books, 2006).

3. Naomi Ragen's novel *Jephte's Daughter* (New York: Warner Books, 1989), however, describes a girl who was always made happy by the story of Abraham and Isaac. It was "her favorite story." The novel is quoted in Juengst, *Sharing Faith with Children*, pp. 88–89. Children are individuals and will respond differently to any story we tell.

4. De la Mare, *Early One Morning in the Spring*, p. 270.

5. See Dianne E. Deming, *A Time with Our Children: Stories for Use in Worship, Year A* (Cleveland: The Pilgrim Press, 1992), pp. 95–97.

6. Andersen, *The Complete Fairy Tales and Stories*, pp. 386–89.

7. Raymond MacDonald Alden, *Why the Chimes Rang* (Indianapolis: Guild Press, 1994); Shel Silverstein, *The Giving Tree* (New York: Harper & Row, 1964); Doris Stickney, *Water Bugs and Dragonflies: Explaining Death to Young Children*, rev. ed. (Cleveland: The Pilgrim Press, 2004); Margaret Wise Brown, *The Runaway Bunny* (New York: Harper & Row, 1972 [c. 1942]).

8. Andersen, *The Complete Fairy Tales and Stories*, pp. 1004, 1053.

9. Frederick Buechner, *The Clown in the Belfry: Writings on Faith and Fiction* (San Francisco: HarperSanFrancisco, 1992), p. 57.

10. University of California, http://calbears.collegesports.com/genrel/043098aaa.html (accessed September 14, 2006); St. Petersburg Times, http://www.sptimes.com/News/92699/Sports/_Wrong_Way_Riegels_t.shtml (accessed September 12, 2006). Lauren Winner tells another effective story about a second chance. Forced by her mother to return a quarter she had taken while tidying her kindergarten teacher's desk drawer, she was forgiven for taking it and then surprised soon after when the teacher asked her—"a desk-drawer quarter thief"—if she would like to tidy the desk drawer again. See Lauren F. Winner, *Girl Meets God: On the Path to a Spiritual Life* (Chapel Hill, NC: Algonquin Books of Chapel Hill, 2002), pp. 206–7.

11. I heard a tape of Johnson telling the story at a National Park Service presentation at the Johnson ranch in Texas, a National Historical Park, in 1986.

12. Harold Steindam, *Bearing Fruit: Sermons for Children* (Cleveland: United Church Press, 1994), pp. 6–7.

13. Baker, *Let the Children Come*, pp. 21–22, 56–57.

14. Dann, *Creating Children's Sermons*, pp. 83–84.

15. Philip D. Schroeder, *Children's Sermons for the Revised Common Lectionary, Year A: Using the 5 Senses to Tell God's Story* (Nashville: Abingdon Press, 1997), p. 47.

16. Philip Sidney, *An Apology for Poetry or The Defence of Poesy*, ed. Geoffrey Shepherd (London: Thomas Nelson and Sons, 1965), p. 113.

17. Hans Christian Anderson used this phrase in his story "The Bell Deep." See *The Complete Fairy Tales and Stories*, p. 589. Hugh Lofting began *The Story of Dr. Dolittle* (New York: William Morrow and Co., 1997), p. 1, in a similar way: "Once upon a time, many years ago—

when our grandfathers were little children. . . ."

18. Elias Bredsdorff, *Hans Christian Andersen: The Story of His Life and Work, 1805-75* (New York: Charles Scribner's Sons, 1975), pp. 300, 346.

19. Ronald B. Mierzwa, *Childchurch: Homily Outlines for Preaching to Children* (San Jose, CA: Resource Publications, Inc., 1996), p. 8.

20. Russell, *Autobiography*, 1:27.

21. Thomas E. Boomershine, *Story Journey: An Invitation to the Gospel as Storytelling* (Nashville: Abingdon, 1988), pp. 39-40.

22. Brent Ashabranner, *The Times of My Life: A Memoir* (New York: Cobblehill Books/Dutton, 1990), pp. 69-70. Various books have been written about storytelling. One I have used is Elaine M. Ward, *The Art of Storytelling* (Brea, CA: Educational Ministries, 1990). A brief but insightful guide is Jay O'Callaghan's "Thoughts on Storytelling" in McNulty's *Preaching Better*, pp. 30-36.

CHAPTER THIRTEEN: *Conversations*

1. Stewart and Hubner, *Talking about Something Important*, p. 49.

2. Kathleen Bostrom, "I Have Always Believed" in Steven W. Vannoy, ed., *The Greatest Gifts Our Children Give to Us: The Surprising Wisdom of Kids* (New York: Simon & Schuster, 1997), pp. 151-52.

3. Herbert Anderson and Susan B. W. Johnson, *Regarding Children: A New Respect for Childhood and Families* (Louisville, KY: Westminster John Knox Press, 1994), p. 126.

4. Sonja M. Stewart and Jerome W. Berryman, *Young Children and Worship* (Louisville, KY: Westminster/John Knox Press, 1989), pp. 16, 30-31.

5. Gerard A. Pottebaum, *To Walk with a Child: Homiletics for Children: A Guide* (Loveland, OH: Treehaus Communications, Inc., 1993), pp. 132-35.

6. Steindam, *Bearing Fruit*, pp. 114-15.

7. Harold Steindam, letter to author, May 27, 2004.

8. Anna Jameson, *A Commonplace Book of Thoughts, Memories, and Fancies, Original and Selected* (London: Longman, Brown, Green, and Longmans, 1854), pp. 234-35.

9. Karris Golden, "Sharp-witted Chippy Plays Pastor's Sidekick in Children's Ministry," *Waterloo-Cedar Falls, Iowa, Courier*, Dec. 14, 1998; Samuel H. Fountain, "Serendipity—Story Communicates the Gospel: An Experiment in Children Participating in the Development and Writing of 'Children's

Sermons," (DMin professional project, Theological School of Drew University, 1982), p. 113; Fay Quanstrom, "Overhearing the Gospel: The Value of Children's Messages for the Congregation in All-age Worship" (DMin thesis, Northern Baptist Theological Seminary, 1998), pp. 9-10.

10. Matthias Kleis, "Arbeitsbuch: Methoden der Kinderpredigt," pp. 22-26 (Puppenspiel). Pastoralweb, http://pastoralweb.de /Kinderpredigt/Kinderpredigt.PDF (accessed September 14, 2006)

CHAPTER FOURTEEN: *Interruptions*

1. Dann, *Creating Children's Sermons*, p. 51.

EPILOGUE: *Sowers*

1. Scott Davis Youngblood, "Inclusiveness: The Incorporation of Elementary Age Children in the Total Morning Worship Experience: Development, Implementation, and Evaluation of an Educational Model for St. John's United Methodist Church, Georgetown, Texas" (DMin professional project, Perkins School of Theology, Southern Methodist University, 1992), p. 83.

2. Walter Esaias Reifsnyder, "An Analysis of Children's Sermons" (PhD thesis, University of Pittsburgh, 1937), pp. 22-45.

3. Edward P. Smith, *Gerty's Papa's Civil War*, ed. William H. Armstrong (New York: The Pilgrim Press, 1984), p. xiii.

4. William H. Armstrong, *A Friend to God's Poor: Edward Parmelee Smith* (Athens, GA: University of Georgia Press, 1993), p. 180.

5. Ibid.

6. Robert Coles, *The Story of Ruby Bridges* (New York: Scholastic, 1995), unnumbered p. 22.

7. Coles, *The Moral Life of Children*, pp. 9, 22-26. See also his article, "The Inexplicable Prayers of Ruby Bridges," in Kelly Monroe, ed., *Finding God at Harvard: Spiritual Journeys of Thinking Christians* (Grand Rapids, MI: Zondervan Publishing House, 1996), pp. 33-40.

8. Henry B. Gonzalez, "Remarks of U.S. Representative Henry B. Gonzalez, John F. Kennedy Library, September 11, 1994," John F. Kennedy Library, Boston, Mass.

9. Ibid. The original as quoted by Gonzalez is:

Nada te turbe
Nada te espante
Todo se pasa,
La Paciencia todo lo alcanza
Quien a Dios tiene la falta
Solo Dios basta.

APPENDIX A:
Fry Graph for Estimating Readability

1. Zakaluk and Samuels, *Readability: Its Past, Present, and Future*, p. 95.

APPENDIX B: *"The Object Lesson"* by James Whitcomb Riley.

1. Riley, *Complete Works of James Whitcomb Riley*, 9:2480-84.

Bibliography

~

I have attempted to compile as complete a bibliography on children's sermons and preaching to children as I could, including books, articles, and academic studies. I have not, however, included collections of children's sermons unless they contain substantial remarks about the purpose and methodology of the sermons. Nor have I included the many useful books about child development or children and worship.

Adams, Paul M. *The Sermon for Children: A Research Handbook for Church Leaders*. Montello, NV: Paul M. Adams, 1994.

Allen, J. Timothy. "Reconstructing the Children's Sermon." *Preaching* 6 (May-June 1991): 16-20.

Anderson, Deann Halligan. "A Critique of Children's Sermons." MDiv research project, Lexington Theological Seminary, 1986.

Anderson, Phil. "Let the Children Come." *The Topeka Capital-Journal*, Apr. 8, 2000. Topeka Capital-Journal. http://cjonline.com/stories/040800/rel_children.shtml.

Anderson, Victor. "Face to Face: Becoming a Pastor to Children."

Reformed Worship 12 (Summer 1989): 14-15.

Baker, Brant D. *Let the Children Come: A New Approach to Children's Sermons*. Minneapolis: Augsburg, 1991.

——. *Welcoming the Children: Experiential Children's Sermons*. Minneapolis: Augsburg, 1995.

Baker, Brian. "Experiencing the Gospel with Children: A Model for the Children's Sermon Based on the New Homiletic and the Catechesis of the Good Shepherd." DMin thesis, Seabury-Western Theological Seminary, 1999.

Ban, Arline J. *Children's Time in Worship*. Valley Forge, PA: Judson Press, 1981.

Barber, Bob. "Handling Children's Object Lessons." *The Christian Ministry* 18 (Sept.-Oct. 1987): 23-24.

Beecher, Edward. "On Preaching to Children." *The Independent*. June 22, 1871.

Bess, C. W. *Object-centered Children's Sermons*. Grand Rapids, MI: Baker Book House, 1978.

Black, James. "Preaching Children's Sermons." *Monday Morning* 46 (Dec. 20, 1937): 5.

Blevins, Stanley Nance. "The Children's Sermon as a Basis for Spiritual Dialogue between Parents and Children." DMin professional project report, Southwestern Baptist Theological Seminary, 1982.

Bontrager, John Kenneth. "The Story Sermon as a Ministry to

Children and Adults in the Light of Psychological Insight and New Testament Understanding of Parable." DMin professional project, School of Theology at Claremont, California, 1977.

Bowes, Peter. *Children in Church Worship*. Edinburgh: Handsel Press and Rutherford House, 1990.

Brown, Carolyn C. "Preparing to Preach to the Kids." *Preaching* 13 (Sept.-Oct. 1997): 35-40.

——. *You Can Preach to the Kids, Too! Designing Sermons for Adults and Children*. Nashville: Abingdon Press, 1997.

Brown, Danny H. "The Children's Sermon: Proclaiming the Story to Children as an Act of Worship in the Community of Faith." DMin research project, School of Theology and Missions, Oral Roberts University, 1986. (I have not been able to obtain and read this project.)

Campbell, Connie. "Preaching 'To' and 'For' Children." Mercer University, Center for Baptist Studies. http://www.mercer.edu/baptiststudies/conferences/presentations/campbell.htm.

Cancro, Francis T. "To Live the Word with Little Folks." In Frank J. McNulty, ed., *Preaching Better*. New York: Paulist Press, 1985.

Carlson, Robert T., Jr. "Sacred Speech and Children: The Relationship of 'Children's Sermon' and Liturgy." DMin Project, Austin Presbyterian Theological Seminary, 1996.

——. "Sacred Speech and Children: The Relationship of the Children's Sermon and Liturgy." *Journal for Preachers* 23 (Pentecost 2000): 22-24.

Carr, James A. "The Children's Sermon: An Act of Worship for the Community of Faith." *Perkins Journal* 36 (Spring 1983): 1-57.

Case, Charles R. "An Investigation into the Functional Values of the Children's Sermon within the Framework of the Morning Worship Service." DMin thesis-project, Eastern Baptist Theological Seminary, 1981.

"Children's Sermons." *The Christian Ministry* 13 (Jan.1982): 17-20.

"Children's Sermons and Luther's Small Catechism." *Concordia Journal* 15 (Apr. 1989): 100-101.

Cochran, Shelley E. "Let the Children Come: Resources for Including Children in Worship." *Reformed Worship* 27 (Spring 1993): 29-31.

Coffin, Henry Sloane. *The Public Worship of God: A Source Book.* Philadelphia: The Westminster Press, 1946. Chapter 9, "Children and Public Worship" (pp.156-79), is concerned with preaching to children.

Coleman, Richard J. "Beyond Moralism: Children's Sermons Should Bring Good News Rather Than Grand Expectations." *Reformed Worship* 12 (Summer 1989): 10-13.

——. *Gospel-Telling: The Art and Theology of Children's Sermons.* Grand Rapids, MI: William B. Eerdmans Publishing Co., 1982. In 2002, a revised edition was published by CSS Publishing Co. in Lima, Ohio.

——. "Maximizing the Children's Sermon." *Leadership* 7 (Winter 1986): 80-85.

Coombs, Robert Stephen, "A Model for Developing Object Lesson Children's Sermons in the West Hills Baptist Church of Knoxville, TN." DMin thesis, Southern Baptist Theological Seminary, 1988. (I have not been able to obtain and read this thesis.)

Cooper, Paul. "Ministering God's Word to Children." In C. R. Thomas, ed., *Evangelism and the Reformed Faith and Other Essays Commemorating the Ministry of J. Graham Miller*. Sydney: Christian Education Committee Presbyterian Church of Australia, 1980.

Cram, Ronald. "Children and the Language of Preaching." *Journal for Preachers* 17 (Easter 1994): 26–30.

Cross, J. Russell. "Preaching to Children." ThM thesis, Louisville Presbyterian Seminary, 1938.

Dann, Bucky. *Creating Children's Sermons: 51 Visual Lessons*. Philadelphia: The Westminster Press, 1981.

Dann, L. Philip. "Taking Children Seriously." *The Christian Ministry* 16 (Jan. 1985): 11–14.

DeHaven, Charles. "Children's Sermons: Development, Content and Method." DMin dissertation/project, San Francisco Theological Seminary, 1995.

De Ovies, Raimundo. *The Church and the Children*. New York: Morehouse-Gorham Co., 1941.

De Puy, Norman. "Close, But No Cigar." *The Christian Century* 108 (Oct. 23, 1991): 963.

Dickerson, Evelyn J. "Preaching, Teaching, Reaching: Using Narrative with the Lectionary in Preaching and Worship with

Adults and Children." DMin professional paper, Chicago Theological Seminary, 1992.

Dillard, Polly. "Children and Worship." *Review and Expositor* 80 (1983): 261-70.

"Do Sermons to Children Educate?: A Symposium." *Religious Education* 19 (Dec. 1924): 362-96.

Dunbar, Thomas Ashton. "The Children's Sermon: Can the Minister's Awareness of Child Development Principles Strengthen This Experience?" DMin professional project, Theological School of Drew University, 1982.

Etter, John W. *The Preacher and His Sermon: A Treatise on Homiletics.* Dayton, OH: United Brethren Publishing House, 1885. Chapter 6, "Sermons to Children" (pp. 256-81), is concerned with preaching to children.

Faith Lutheran Church, Carthage, MO. "Children's Sermons." Fast Freedom, Inc. http://users.joplin.com/faith/child/htm.

Foster, Charles R. "Proclaiming the Word with Children." *Worship Alive!* Nashville: Discipleship Resources, n.d.

Fountain, Samuel H. "Serendipity—Story Communicates the Gospel: An Experiment in Children Participating in the Development and Writing of 'Children's Sermons.'" DMin professional project, Theological School of Drew University, 1982.

Fowlkes, Mary Anne, and Jennifer Miller. "Proclamation and Children." *Reformed Liturgy and Music* 22 (Winter 1988): 11-15.

Frost, S. B. "The Preacher's Address to the Children." *The Preacher's*

Quarterly (June 1956): 100-107.

Gobbel, A. Roger, and Gertrude G. Gobbel. "Children and Worship." *Religious Education* 74 (Nov.-Dec. 1979): 571-82.

Golden, Karris. "Sharp-witted Chippy Plays Pastor's Sidekick in Children's Ministry." *Waterloo-Cedar Falls, Iowa, Courier*, Dec. 14, 1998.

Grounds, Larry S. "To Such as These: How to Design and Present Children's Stories for Congregational Worship." DMin dissertation project, San Francisco Theological Seminary, 2002.

Henry, H. T. "Preaching to Children." *The Homiletic and Pastoral Review* 42 (Mar. 1942): 510-18.

Hermann, Dolores E. *Preparing Your Own Chapel Talks for Children: Bringing the Word to Little Ones*. St. Louis: Concordia Publishing House, 1987.

Hewitt, Beth Edington. *Captivating Children's Sermons: Crafting Powerful, Practical Messages*. Grand Rapids, MI: Baker Books, 2005.

Hill, John C. *The Children's Sermon. With a Selection of Five Minute Sermons to Children, for Pastors, Sunday-School Libraries and Home Reading*. Philadelphia: Presbyterian Board of Publication, 1882.

Howell, Jefferson Trent, Jr. "To Such Belongs the Kingdom: Children's Sermons: Their Development, Presentation, and Use in Services of Worship." DMin report, Columbia Theological Seminary, 1981.

Huchthausen, John Theodore. "Factors Toward a More Effective Preaching to Children: Ages Five to Nine." BD research paper,

Concordia Theological Seminary, 1967.

Hudnall, Michael Benjamin. "Theoretical and Practical Aspects of the Children's Sermon Today." BD thesis, Divinity School of Duke University, 1949.

Isaacson, Carl. "Telling the Story to Children." *The Christian Ministry* 13 (Sept. 1982): 20-22, 38.

James, Ann. "The Children's Sermon Can Be Effective." *The Christian Ministry* 20 (July-Aug. 1989): 12-15.

Jeffs, H. *The Art of Addressing Children.* London: James Clarke & Co., [1924?].

Jones, D. Raye. "A Child in Their Midst: Strengthening the Children's Sermon." DMin dissertation, Columbia Theological Seminary, 1999.

Jordan, Jerry Marshall. *Filling Up the Brown Bag (A Children's Sermon How-to Book).* Cleveland: The Pilgrim Press, 1987.

Juengst, Sara Covin. *Sharing Faith with Children: Rethinking the Children's Sermon.* Louisville, KY: Westminster John Knox Press, 1994.

Kalas, Steven C. "Children's Sermons: Yuk or Yea?" *Leader in the Church School Today* 2 (Summer 1989): 38-40.

Kelsey, Robert E. "Sheep, Balloons and Beach Balls." *The Christian Ministry* 14 (Nov. 1983): 29-30.

Kleis, Matthias. "Arbeitsbuch: Methoden der Kinderpredigt." Pastoralweb.

http://pastoralweb.de/Kinderpredigt/Kinderpredigt.PDF.

Lanway, Leland Michael. "The Role of the Minister-Child Relationship in the Purpose, Content, and Presentation of the Children's Sermon." ThM thesis, The Southern Baptist Theological Seminary, 1988.

Lewis, J. L., C. J. Maholski, and A. L. Moliere. "Inclusion of Children's Sermons in the Worship Services of Mainline Protestant Denominations." Master's project, Mercer University, 1998. (I have not been able to obtain and read this project.)

Lewis, Richard W. *Preaching to Children*. Nashville: Cumberland Presbyterian Publishing House, [19--?]. The exact date is unknown.

Loscalzo, Craig. "Preachers, Creatures & Children in Church." *The Online Pulpit*. InterVarsity Christian Fellowship. http://www.ivpress.com/churchlink/onlinepulpit/1997-01.php.

Lutheran Church—Missouri Synod, Commission on Worship. "Reflections on Children's Sermons/Messages." Lutheran Worship Notes, Issue #36. The Lutheran Church—Missouri Synod. http://www.lcms.org/pages/internal.asp?NavID=3725.

MacCabe, Maurice. "Preaching to Children." *Christian Standard* 127 (June 14, 1992): 6.

Maison, Jeffrey L. *I Love to Tell the Story*. St. Louis: Chalice Press, 1998.

Maxwell, Jack M. "The Children's Sermon." An unpublished and undated paper graciously furnished to me by the author in 2004.

McEntyre, Marilyn Chandler. "Preaching to Preschoolers." *Christianity Today* 45 (Aug. 6, 2001): 65.

Medlin, William T. III. "Exploring How Children and Their Parents Respond to Various Means of Children's Participation in Worship." DMin professional project, Theological School of Drew University, 1986.

Meissgeier, Ellen. "On Children's Sermons." *Lutheran Partners* 5 (Nov.-Dec. 1989): 30.

Mierzwa, Ronald B. *Childchurch: Homily Outlines for Preaching to Children.* San Jose, CA: Resource Publications, Inc., 1996.

Millett, Craig B. "Giving Children More Than a Sermon." *The Christian Ministry* 20 (July-Aug. 1989): 8-11.

Murray, Don A. "Who Speaks for the Children?" *Lutheran Partners* 5 (Nov.-Dec. 1989): 31.

Neels, Dennis John. "The Potential for Reaching Children Ages One through Twelve in the Sunday Sermon." MDiv research paper, Concordia Theological Seminary, 1973.

Ng, David. "Children's Sermons." In William H. Willimon and Richard Lischer, eds., *Concise Encyclopedia of Preaching.* Louisville, KY: Westminster John Knox Press, 1995, pp. 67-70.

——. "Encouraging Children to Hear the Word of God." *Reformed Liturgy and Music* 26 (Winter 1992): 26-27.

Nichols, Donald N. "Testing the Viability of Using Photographs in the Christian Education of Children, During the Church Hour." DMin professional project, Theological School of Drew

University, 1980.

Nieman, James. "Three Thuds, Four D's, and a Rubik's Cube of Children's Sermons." *Currents in Theology and Mission* 22 (Aug. 1995): 259-63.

Odebunmi, Emmanuel Olaleke. "Developing an Effective Children's Worship in a Local Church." DMin project report, Golden Gate Baptist Theological Seminary, 1982.

Osmer, Richard R. "Teaching the Catechism in the Children's Sermon: A New Possibility for Biblical and Theological Literacy." *Journal for Preachers* 22 (Pentecost 1999): 37-43.

Pecota, Daniel B. "Except You Become as Little Children: An Exploratory Project in Preparing Pastors to Preach to Children." DMin field project report, Graduate Seminary of Phillips University, 1973.

Pottebaum, Gerard A. *To Walk with a Child: Homiletics for Children. A Guide.* Loveland, OH: Treehaus Communications, Inc., 1993.

Quanstrom, Fay. "Overhearing the Gospel: The Value of Children's Messages for the Congregation in All-Age Worship." DMin thesis, Northern Baptist Theological Seminary, 1998.

Rabus, Siegfried. *Die Kinderpredigt: Problem und Bestand einer kindgemässen Sprache der Kirche.* Hamburg: Furche-Verlag, 1967.

Rainsley, Glen E. *Small Wonders: Sermons for Children.* Cleveland: United Church Press, 1998.

Reifsnyder, Walter Esaias. "An Analysis of Children's Sermons." PhD thesis, University of Pittsburgh, 1937.

Roads, Charles. *Little Children in the Church of Christ*. Boston: D. Lothrop Co., 1893.

Rogness, Michael. "Children's Sermons? Yes!" *Word and World* 10 (Winter 1990): 57, 59.

Rossman, Parker. "Children Who Listen." *The Christian Ministry* 16 (Jan. 1985): 15-17.

Rowins, Charles. "Measuring the Effectiveness of Preaching in Parables." DMin thesis project report, Princeton Theological Seminary, 1987. (The project was based on work with sixth-grade children.)

Sassaman, Dick. "How to Give a Successful Children's Sermon." *Church Management* (Mar. 1970): 15.

Schroeder, Philip Daniel. "From Illustration to Animation: Modeling a Paradigm Shift in Worship and Homiletics through Children's Sermons." DMin thesis, United Theological Seminary, 1995.

Scott, Jeffery Warren. "The Awesome Power of the Children's Sermon." *Preacher's Magazine* 73 (Dec. 1997): 24-25.

Sharp, John K. *Teaching and Preaching Religion to Children: A Handbook of Practical Procedure for Those Who Instruct the Young in Religion*. New York: P. J. Kenedy and Sons, 1936.

Sims, O. Suthern, Jr. "Children's Worship: Empirical Research Findings on the Children's Sermon and Suggestions for Implementation." *Review and Expositor* 96 (Fall 1999): 549-64.

———. *Creating and Leading Children's Sermons: A Developmental Approach*. Macon, GA: Smyth & Helwys, 1999.

[Smith, Debra D.] "Leading Children's Moments." Office of Children's Ministry, United Methodist General Board of Discipleship, 1998.

Smith, Hugh III. "Creating Children's Stories that Work in Worship for Children and the Child Within." DMin thesis project report, Princeton Theological Seminary, 1992.

Smith, Theron Walker, Jr. "Using the Narrative Approach to Preaching in Children's Sermons during Advent." DMin report, Candler School of Theology, Emory University, 1987.

Smith, W. Alan. "The Child in the Body of Christ: Inclusive Children's Sermons in the Worshiping Community." DMin project, Divinity School of Vanderbilt University, 1983.

——. *Children Belong in Worship: A Guide to the Children's Sermon.* St. Louis: CBP Press, 1984.

Staigers, Del. "Let the Little Children Come to Me: Preaching the Gospel to Children." *Catholic Education* 4 (Sept. 2000): 90–103.

Steindam, Harold. *Bearing Fruit: Sermons for Children.* Cleveland: United Church Press, 1994.

Stewart, Stan, and Pauline Hubner. *Talking about Something Important.* Melbourne: The Joint Board of Christian Education of Australia and New Zealand, 1981.

Stillings, Gildon D. "Children's Sermons: Communicating with the Congregation." DMin project report, Boston University School of Theology, 1985.

Stocking, Jay T. *The Child in the Congregation.* Boston: The Pilgrim

Press, 1929.

Tiemann, Ray. "The Gospel Message for All God's Children: Deepening Faith across Generations through the Interaction between the Children's and Adult Sermons." DMin professional paper, The Lutheran School of Theology at Chicago, 1995.

Tostengard, Sheldon. "Children's Sermons? No!" *Word and World* 10 (Winter 1990): 56, 58.

Trull, Joe E. "How to Give a Children's Sermon." *Proclaim* 8 (Oct. 1977): 42, 48.

Trumbull, H. Clay. *The Sunday-School: Its Origin, Mission, Methods, and Auxiliaries*. Philadelphia: John D. Wattles & Co., 1896. These are the Lyman Beecher Lectures before Yale Divinity School for 1888. Lectures 9 and 10 (pp. 309-77) are on preaching to children.

Van Dyk, Wilbert M. "Preach the Word! To Children?" *Calvin Theological Journal* 32 (Nov. 1997): 431-43.

——. "'Will All the Children Please Come Forward?': Uses and Abuses of the Children's Sermon." *Reformed Worship* 36 (June 1995): 24-25.

Van Gessel, Douglas. "The Principles and Practice of Preaching to Children from the Pulpit." ThM thesis, Northern Baptist Theological Seminary, 1965.

Van Ormer, A. B. Bunn. *Ministering to Boys and Girls*. Burlington, IA: The Lutheran Literary Board, 1933.

Weaver, Andrew J. "Children's Sermons Are Fun." *The Christian Ministry* 10 (July 1979): 23.

Weisheit, Eldon. *God's Word in a Child's World: Messages and Guidelines for Sharing the Gospel with Children.* Minneapolis: Augsburg Publishing House, 1986.

Welz, Stefan. *Die Kinderpredigt: Zur Predigtlehre und Praxis eines Verkündigungsmodells.* Hooksiel: Jade Verlag, 2001. Welz's bibliography includes other recent works on children's sermons in German.

Wester, Donald Ray. "Preparing Adults to Preach with Children." DMin thesis project, Aquinas Institute of Theology, 2001.

"When Do Your Children Hear a Sermon?" *Christian Standard* 126 (Jan. 13, 1991): 3.

Willimon, William H. "Children's Sermons Are Not the Answer." *Circuit Rider* 58 (Sept. 1981): 12-13.

——. "Keep Them in Their Place?" *Worship Alive!* Nashville: Discipleship Resources, n.d.

——. "Preaching to Children." *Faith and Mission* 3 (Fall 1985): 24-31.

Youngblood, Scott Davis. "Inclusiveness: The Incorporation of Elementary Age Children in the Total Morning Worship Experience: Development, Implementation, and Evaluation of an Educational Model for St. John's United Methodist Church, Georgetown, Texas." DMin professional project, Perkins School of Theology, Southern Methodist University, 1992.

Zalesak, Richard Joseph, Sr. "The Training of Lay Preachers for Children's Sermons." DMin thesis, Gordon-Conwell Theological Seminary, Charlotte, N.C., 1999.

Acknowledgments

~

I want to thank the many people who helped me during my study of children's sermons.

Two librarians were of special help to me in locating information about children's sermons: Kevin L. Smith, formerly assistant librarian at the Methodist Theological School in Ohio in Delaware, Ohio, and now director of the Pilgrim Library at Defiance College in Defiance, Ohio; and Richard Berg, director of the Philip Schaff Library at Lancaster Theological Seminary in Lancaster, Pennsylvania. Richard Berg and his wife, Judy, also proved to be gracious hosts during a visit to Lancaster.

The staff of the Cuyahoga County Public Library in Cuyahoga County, Ohio, patiently filled my many requests for loans from other libraries.

Two other libraries with liberal lending policies for patrons living at a distance were helpful in providing me with books and articles: the Congregational Library in Boston, Massachusetts, and the Kesler Circulating Library, a service of the Divinity Library of Vanderbilt University in Nashville, Tennessee.

The authors cited in the bibliography stimulated my thinking, as did the many authors of collections of children's sermons I read and the various preachers I observed as I thought about the purpose of children's sermons and the methods of preaching them.

Several people read the book in manuscript. Their comments, from a variety of disciplines, were a great help to me in improving it. I want to thank those readers: Fredericka Berger; Margaret Borrelli; Lawrence H. Craig; Elizabeth Cupp; D. Ray Heisey; Rodney L. Mundy; Harold Steindam; and Jacob B. Wagner.

Finally, many children have taught me simply by being who they are, especially my grandchildren: Conner and Cara Kasten; and Louisa, Graham, and Olivia Armstrong.